REGISTERING THE HUMAN TERRAIN:
A VALUATION OF CADASTRE

Douglas E. Batson

NDIC PRESS

The National Defense Intelligence College supports and encourages research on intelligence issues that distills lessons and improves Intelligence Community capabilities to policy-level and operational consumers

This book is the culmination of research by Douglas Batson while he was an Office of the Director of National Intelligence Research Fellow at this College in 2006-2007. The manuscript was originally prepared to fulfill part of the requirements for Research Fellows at this institution. Mr. Batson's work offers specifics on how to assist developing countries in registering property so the owners have security of tenure. Property rights are at the heart of many problems in dealing with refugees and in turn with governmental stability. Its publication offers an example of the variety of applied intelligence research carried out by the Research Fellows.

This publication is based on open sources, and the views expressed are those of the author. The views do not necessarily reflect the official policy or position of the Department of Defense or the U.S. Government.

Photographs and graphics from the American Geographical Society, the Association of American Geographers, from the Land Titling and Economic Reconstruction Activity (LTERA-Afghanistan), as well as from the Emerging Markets Group (EMG) and the Terra Institute are used by permission. Photos and maps from the Mexico Indigena Project are used courtesy of the University of Kansas.

Distribution of this publication is unrestricted. Paper copies are available in limited quantities to individuals in the Intelligence Community and to other U.S. Government officials through the Center for Strategic Intelligence Research of the College. Electronic copies of this and other Center publications are available via the Worldwide Web at http://www.ndic.edu. For more information on this or other publications email the Center's Associate Director at *james.lightfoot@ dia.mil* or phone 202-231-1917.

ii

Dr. James E. Lightfoot
Editor and Associate Director,
Center for Strategic Intelligence Research

CONTENTS

CONTENTS (Continued)

FOREWORD

I first met Doug Batson at the National Geospatial-Intelligence Agency's Washington Navy Yard location in 2005, before he was honored with the award leading to the research and publication of this book. We shared an intellectual passion in our work with human terrain analytical issues and I came to respect Doug as someone I could learn from.

Doug's subsequent selection as an Office of the Director of National Intelligence Rearch Fellow was well deserved. *Registering the Human Terrain: A Valuation of Cadastre* validates this selection. The scholarship that follows is worthy of both study and careful reflection; this work is a must-read for those engaging in research, analysis, and policy development regarding the important issues of cadastre and human terrain analysis more generally.

As Doug points out in his preface, while many in the community have been focused on the "where" relating to mapping the human terrain, this book tackles the important issue of *who* is registered to land through property records. Mapping the human terrain, of course, would be greatly aided by the collection, processing, and analysis of the kind of data Doug advocates, but the work here goes beyond the furthering of the emerging discipline of human terrain analysis to broader strategic and policy environments. Clearly, the case is made for furthering efforts in registering the human terrain as a means to achieving goals of national security and global peace and stability.

As Doug's work lays out, land issues are often at the core of violent conflict, which could be prevented by the development and implementation of land registration systems with formal mechanisms to arbitrate disputes and make public record of land ownership rights and adjudications. The United States can lead by assisting developing countries to develop such systems for land tenure and property rights. This assistance would be much less controversial than much of our current foreign policy. This systemization of land tenure and property rights would do much for the national security of our country, as it is increasingly dependent upon the stability of the developing world.

Doug's work here is timely and a harbinger of policy shifts to come. As the United States government organizes and re-organizes itself to address conflict resolution and promote global stability, we will increasingly recognize the value of the human terrain. *Registering the Human Terrain: A Valuation of*

Cadastre will serve many as an introduction to the importance of cadastral data and a way ahead to leverage the power of it.

Dr. Swen Johnson
Chief of Human Terrain Analysis
Socio-Cultural Intelligence Analysis, Inc.
Alexandria, VA

COMMENTARY

Mr. Yaïves Ferland
Defense Research and Development
Canada at Valcartier (DRDC-Valcartier)

There are three main aspects of prime interest in Douglas Batson's book about cadastre as a method to help create a peaceful and productive civil society after conflicts and the return of refugees. First, for the defence and security intelligence community, it represents a step forward in both the comprehension and the application of the socio-cultural and economic dimensions of any conflict: the structure of relationships to the land. The role of land ownership in the fields and in cities as a conflict catalyst is discussed extensively. Land is fundamental for all societies and eras, but there are dozens of complicated meanings and circumstances from the parcel-lot and dwelling, the soil, and the ground-related activities and culture, to the terrain to exploit and the homeland territory to secure. Land crises can lead to conquests, depressions, revolutions, and reforms, but often conflicts provoke crises by physical destruction or population expulsion, separation, concentration, or return. For intelligence to reach situation awareness, one needs to understand the dynamic of such relationships to land, beyond the physical terrain, as arguments in an actual conflict.

Second, Batson explores the deep significance of the cadastre as a formidable institution that permits security for a fragile population and its recovering economy. In any cases, by any means, even temporary titling and registration of land allocation or possession contribute to security, at many levels of Maslow's pyramid. If well-established and adapted to both traditional and innovative views of land definition, measurement, identification, registration, and conveyance, the cadastre informs and aids effective reconstruction, peacemaking, and control of speculation. Cadastre is not a universal cure and no definition is globally accepted, even among land-surveyors or planners; the cadastre is subject to controversy depending on the origins of structural problems to address in different countries, and with respect to various legal systems concerning property and land market. Batson brings in his experience in post-conflict Afghanistan to discuss the crucial role of the cadastre in land administration policies and institutions.

Third, this contribution fits well at the vanguard of a revitalized military geography. Chapters directly engage in the rehabilitation of the geographer's perspective for improved land conflict and policy considerations. It is no more a question only of geopolitics or geostrategy (which are not military by essence), it is full geography as defined by the relationships of humans to the Earth. Geography, a basis of military doctrines for decades since Clausewitz, but reduced to popular travelogues, for a while considered useful only in the form of accurate topographic maps, is recovering its standing within defence, security, intelligence, and policy scientific domains. Geographical methods and analysis provide more than information and knowledge about a geospatially complex situation; they include a conceptual reference and expertise frame for addressing land crises and building a stable land administration model, as a cadastre.

COMMENTARY

Lt Col Hennie Janse van Rensburg
South African Military Academy

Batson has produced an easily readable book with a clear theme: effective land administration is pivotal to sustainable Reconstruction and Stability (R&S) in post-conflict societies. A link is established between land and its potential for conflict, as well as how an appropriate land administration system can assist in managing and preventing such conflict. Without a functioning, practical, culturally sensitive and locally calibrated land administration system, sustainable R&S will be exceedingly difficult, if not impossible, to achieve. He proposes focusing R&S efforts on creating a current cadastre of the post-conflict area using a combination of top-down planning and community participation. The reasoning behind this is that such a cadastre:

 a. Is required for an effective land administration system and provides a platform on which nation-building can take place;

 b. Provides a platform for securing land tenure, which is fundamental to building peace and stability within a society;

 c. Provides a platform for solving local land disputes before they escalate to violent conflict, thus assisting in maintaining peace;

 d. Is sustainable because it is embedded in the societal fabric of the area.

Policy makers and R&S specialists will do well to read this book and take note of Batson's arguments. The book is written with a U.S. audience in mind as is evident in Chapter 7: Geography as a Mainstay of U.S. Foreign Policy, as well as in the use of Afghanistan as a case study. Having said that, the book should appeal to all countries faced with reintegrating displaced persons into their own societies, land restitution issues or having to manage R&S, both inside and outside their national boundaries.

A secondary theme that Batson expounds is the importance of geographic knowledge in relation to foreign intelligence, in the setting of appropriate foreign policy as well as establishing and maintaining peace. Considering myself a geographer, Batson surely scores high on my card on this count. Bias aside, good knowledge of human and physical geography leads to better understanding of the international political arena and Batson does well to remind the reader thereof. Of course, this secondary theme would be totally out of place in this book if it did not somehow relate to the main theme – which it does so very clearly. An essential part of a cadastre is the geographic description of the land contained in it. Such a description answers the fundamentally important question: where? Without the answer to this simple geographic question a cadastre cannot exist. Taking this into consideration, geographic knowledge becomes a cornerstone in building peace and stability in post-conflict societies.

A key to the success of any R&S operation is sustainability. If a cadastre is to be sustainable it has to be integrated into and accepted by the local community. Batson demonstrates a much-needed sensitivity in considering the needs of local communities in establishing a cadastre. He aptly notes that the *"... problem in post-conflict societies is that cadastres have been designed to serve the interests of governments and outside powers, not the local people, who are usually poor."* In order for a cadastre to be successful it must be designed keeping the end user in mind. This begs an important question: who is the end user? Is it the society under reconstruction or the society driving the reconstruction? Colonial expansion into Africa in the late 1800s and first half of the 1900s provided Africa with infrastructure such as dirt roads, railroads and harbours. Unfortunately, these infrastructural developments were geared towards resource extraction and not the development of the local communities. Very little local development resulted from the new infrastructure during colonialism and also proved hopelessly inadequate for development in the post-colonial era. The U.S. faces a similar situation in Afghanistan and Iraq. Expediency is one of the biggest Delila's that the U.S. government is currently facing in the Middle East. An expedient, top-down approach that is focused on the need of the U.S. government, instead of the countries under reconstruction, will result in a situation similar to the African colonial experience. The cadastre resulting from such an approach will not be sustainable and neither will the peace be. The U.S. must show patience in engaging the local population in order to establish a cadastre that is culturally sensitive and locally calibrated — as encouraged by Batson.

COMMENTARY

Dr. John Peaty
Defence Geographic Centre
Ministry of Defence, United Kingdom

Douglas Batson, a National Geospatial-Intelligence Agency Regional Analyst and a staff member to the U.S. Board on Geographic Names, has researched and written a study which he has titled "Registering the Human Terrain: A Valuation of Cadastre." He has looked in detail at the case of Afghanistan and the study could well have retained its name from the original proposal, "The Repatriation of 4.6 million Afghan Refugees: Answering the Where Question with Property Intelligence."

Coalition intelligence agencies have learnt and are continuing to learn many hard lessons in Iraq and Afghanistan to include the uncomfortable truths that cultural factors were under-appreciated and that cultural knowledge and awareness were lacking and/or not used effectively. As a result, the IC is now rightly preoccupied with "Mapping the Human Terrain."

But as Batson correctly points out, one must first "Register the Human Terrain." He argues that the "cadastre" is the key to predicting and responding to global crises, a point well-known in Europe but virtually unknown in the U.S. I believe Batson has written an important, valuable and timely study of the crucial problem of land tenure and property rights in Afghanistan. I further believe that his conclusions have a far wider application, well beyond Afghanistan.

Batson further argues that the European-developed Land Administration Domain Model is compelling because it makes explicit the various types of land rights, restrictions, and responsibilities. It may well record land tenure types not based on the traditional cadastral parcel.

In his conclusion Batson puts forward practical recommendations: Recognize the importance of land in conflict prevention; Expand the definition of national security to include security of land tenure; Construct states capable of administering land; Build local capacity in resolving land conflict. His specific suggestions on how to engage multiple actors in land-related reconstruction and stability activities are especially commendable.

I was privileged to collaborate with Batson by reviewing his drafts (and met with him at the International Conference on Military Geography and Geology (ICMGG)). He is to be congratulated for researching and writing this study and the National Defense Intelligence College is to be congratulated for making it publicly available.

AUTHOR'S PREFACE

Living and working for the U.S. Department of the Army in Germany from 1979 to 1992, I observed world-changing geopolitical tensions and triumphs: the deployment of intermediate-range nuclear weapons in that country, the tearing down of the Berlin Wall, and German reunification. As I observed the refitting of a recently-closed U.S. military base into a German government asylum processing center, with barracks for thousands of Eurasian and African refugees instead of American soldiers, I unknowingly witnessed the transition from Cold War stasis to an era marked by unprecedented global migration. My later career, full-time at the then-U.S. Immigration and Naturalization Service, and part-time in the U.S. Army Reserve, and attending successive U.S. Central Command Southwest Asia symposia, alerted me that the mass displacement of people is due largely to land conflict. My selection as an Office of the Director

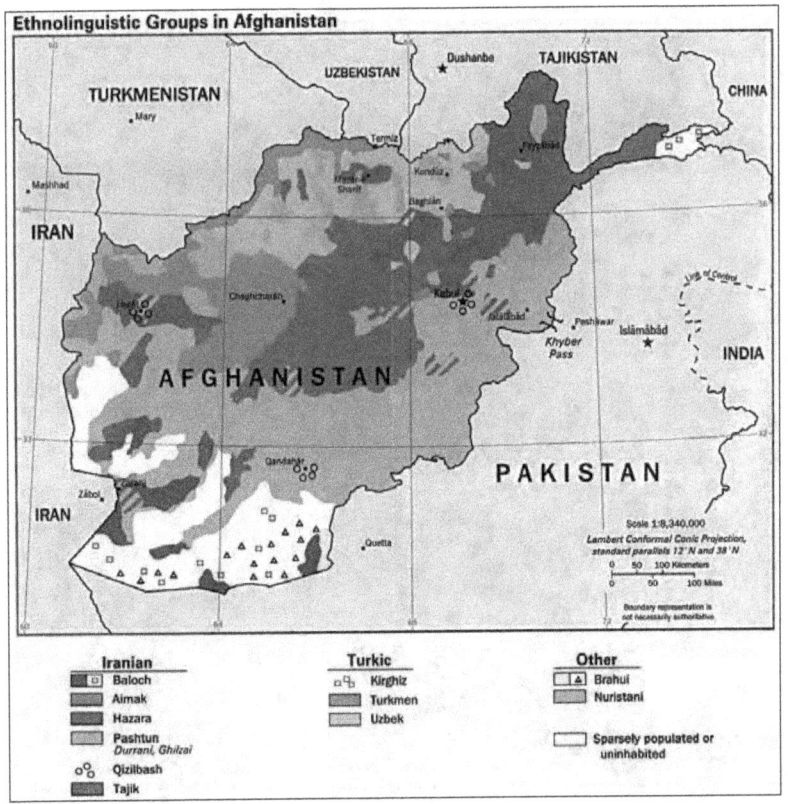

Figure 1. A Map of Afghanistan's Ethnic Mix. *Source: CIA, 1997.*

of National Intelligence Fellow allowed me to research the topic of "Registering the Human Terrain."

A term now in vogue to describe the rendering of socio-cultural information to a map is "mapping the human terrain," which is also an intelligence topic of increasing salience. Ethno-linguistic maps, such as Figure 1 depicting languages spoken or religions practiced in a given area, are plentiful.

However, this book is NOT about mapping the human terrain, but about *registering the human terrain:* tying a "person," an individual, a group, or a non-natural person such as an organization, to a geographical place through property records. This book manifests how to answer the "who" question with the same precision the U.S. Intelligence Community answers the "where" question.

In addition to offering intelligence value, strengthening land tenure and property rights in volatile countries is an auspicious field of international development for the U.S. to assert its "soft power." I am grateful for the time my

xiv

Figure 2. 1:1000 Scale Parcel-based Cadastral Map, Kabul, Afghanistan. *Source: Emerging Markets Group (EMG).*

Figure 3. Persons Tied to a Cadastral Parcel. *Source: Bhuvana Anand, EMG.*

Washington-based U.S. government colleagues, a very small cadre of land tenure and property rights practitioners, took to educate me on their unsung work and to review my drafts. Thank you to Dr. Jolyne Sanjak, Senior Director, Property Rights and Land Tenure Operations at the Millennium Challenge Corporation; Mr. Greg Garramone, Economic Policy Advisor in the Department of State, Office of the Coordinator for Reconstruction and Stability, and Dr. Gregory Myers, Senior Land Tenure and Property Rights Specialist, U.S. Agency for International Development. I trust that this book will attract a new generation of land tenure and property rights experts into your ranks. Many thanks also to:

Dr. J. David Stanfield of the Terra Institute, Mount Horeb, Wisconsin, USA, whose passion for land tenure and property rights and years of labor in Afghanistan is inspiring. His interest in my study, reviews of my drafts, and introductions to his Afghan colleagues prior to my research trip to Afghanistan were invaluable.

Figure 4. The Author.

In Afghanistan, to Engineer M. Yasin Safar, retired chief of the Afghan Geodesy and Cartography Head Office cadastral department; Ms. Rebecca Gang, former Project Coordinator in Herat of the Norwegian Refugee Council's Information, Counseling, and Legal Assistance program; Dr. Gregory Maassen, Chief of Party, Emerging Markets Group Land Titling and Economic Restructuring (EMG) project, for the time and effort to show me EMG's endeavors on the ground; to Mr. Gregg Badger, National Geospatial-Intelligence Agency (NGA), for the daily logistical support in Kabul.

In the Netherlands, to Prof. dr. ir. Peter van Oosterom and Mr. dr. ir. Jaap Zevenbergen, associate professor, both with the OTB Research Institute for Housing, Urban and Mobility Studies, Delft University of Technology, and to Ir. Christiaan Lemmen, assistant professor at the International Institute of Geo-Information Science and Earth Observation (ITC) at Enschede, and vice chair, administration of International Federation of Surveyors Commission 7 "Cadastre and Land Management," for bending your respective schedules to accommodate my visit while en route to Afghanistan, and for introducing me to an opportune cadastral model.

For editing my multiple drafts, Dr. James Lightfoot, Center for Strategic Intelligence Research, National Defense Intelligence College; Dr. Joel Kalvesmaki, U.S. Government Printing Office, and Mr. Yaïves Ferland, Defence Research and Development Canada, Valcartier, Quebec.

For pointing me in the right direction after receiving the DNI Award, my former U.S. Geological Survey colleague, John Moeller.

For encouragement from my home office, the NGA's Political Geography Division: Glen Lauber, Brian Hagan, David Eldridge, Jennifer Faraon, Dr. Peter Viechnicki; from elsewhere in NGA: Randy Flynn, Al Human, Bruce Kiracofe, Dr. Virgil S. "Steve" Lewis, Carter Edgeworth, Adrian Gomes, Tim Mclendon, Brian Pope, and Wendy Zeller.

I thank my loving and supportive wife, Terri, who greeted news of the fellowship award with excitement just three months after we had wed, and who labored arduously on the footnotes and bibliography.

CHAPTER 1:
Introduction

Seldom does an alert of potentially cataclysmic humanitarian crises occur in open-source press releases. An exception occurred in early 2007, in a little-reported story whose headline ran: "All Afghan Refugees to be Repatriated from Pakistan by 2009."[1] The announcement, made by the Pakistani government, foreshadows events that will no doubt parallel those already underway in Iran, where 100,000 unregistered Afghan migrants were deported in a six-week period.[2] Yet, neither Iran's stepped-up deportations of its one million illegal Afghan migrants nor the announced Pakistani strategy for sending back its remaining 2.4 million Afghan refugees by the end of 2009 has been met with alarm.

Alarm is the appropriate response to this impending scenario, since every mass deportation of similar size in the last century—Armenians from Ottoman Turkey during World War I and Chechens to Central Asia under Stalin—has been a recipe for further conflict even generations later. An astute regional analyst would have anticipated Pakistan's preparations to deport its Afghan refugees. First, a four-month, by-name registration campaign of Afghan refugees living in Pakistan, completed in February 2007, identified 88 percent of the refugee population.[3] Second, several decades-old Afghan refugee camps in Pakistan were closed in 2007.[4] Third, the Pakistani government has reiterated that after 15 April 2007, Afghans with no Proof of Registration Cards will be subject to the laws of the land—deportation.[5]

The international community regards forced repatriation as a violation of international law. But Pakistan is not a signatory to the 1951 Convention Relating to the Status of Refugees and subsequent protocols. Even if it were, the Pakistani government might have ignored this commitment and pursued its current

---

1 Syed Irfan Raza, "All Afghans to Be Repatriated by '09," *DAWN Group of Newspapers*, online edition, 16 February 2007.

2 "Afghans Protest Eviction of Refugees by Iran," *Hong Kong AFP in English — Hong Kong service of the independent French press agency Agence France-Press (AFP)e*, online edition, no. JPP20070501969040 Hong Kong AFP in English 0952 GMT, 1 May 2007.

3 "Second Generation Afghan Refugees Prefer Living in Pakistan," *Lahore Daily Times*, online English edition, no. SAP2007030527002, 5 March 2007. Cited hereafter as "Second Generation Afghan Refugees."

4 "Over 200,000 Afghan Refugees Said to Leave Pakistan after Deadline Expiry," *Associated Press of Pakistan (APP)*, online edition, no. 20070424950088 Islamabad APP in English, 24 April 2007. Cited hereafter as "Over 200,000 Afghan Refugees."

5 "Over 200,000 Afghan Refugees."

Figure 5. Internally Displaced Refugees Arrive at Destination. *Source: Photo courtesy of Luke Powell, http://www.lukepowell.com.*

policy, to forcibly deport the estimated 1.5 million Pakistan-born refugees who will not return voluntarily to an Afghanistan they have never known.[6] Since 2002, three million Afghans have repatriated from Pakistan to an Afghanistan ill-suited to absorb them.[7] Another 2.4 million refugees pushed onto its borders would likely trigger a large-scale humanitarian crisis; the reversal of many hard-won gains from Afghanistan's six-year, United States (U.S.)-led reconstruction; and renewed conflicts over land, housing, and other land-related rights, conflicts that the Taliban and anti-coalition militias would immediately exploit.

The refugee crisis brewing in Afghanistan is the most vivid example of a threat to regional stability, world peace, and national sovereignty, concerns that fall under the purview of intelligence analysts and civil reconstruction specialists. The crisis is slowly but inevitably unfolding, and U.S. civil and military planners are inadequately prepared to deal with a titanic reordering of the human terrain.

One of the critical omissions in U.S. efforts to anticipate and then address regional conflicts is the failure to appreciate the relationship between people and their land, information typically registered in a cadastre. For example, spikes in property transactions, inexplicable from market forces alone, can

2 |

---

6 "Second Generation Afghan Refugees."

7 "Over 3 Million Afghans Helped by UN for Repatriation from Pakistan since 2002," *Islamabad Associated Press of Pakistan in English — government-run press agency,* online edition, no. IAP20070409950077 Islamabad APP in English 1250 GMT, 9 April 2007.

indicate escalating criminal activity or ethnic tensions. For the U.S. Intelligence Community, analysis of heretofore unavailable layers of cadastral data has the potential to identify a group's ideologies and economic pillars. By tying a name to a place a cadastre can answer the difficult "who" question: who is behind a given problem? A cadastre can also provide military commanders with detailed knowledge of the human terrain, identification of power brokers on the ground whose support or obstruction may determine mission success. More specifically, this book tells U.S. civil and military planners how cadastral information, where it exists and where it has been maintained, might improve multi-lateral reconstruction and stability (R&S) efforts. Especially in post-conflict societies, land tenure and property rights (LTPR) are a much larger issue; a cadastre is one of many solutions through which stability and peace can return. Conversely, by assigning land ownership or rights to one claimant, a cadastre can extinguish de facto rights and unleash further conflict by empowering a *nouveau* elite at the expense of other claimants. Thus, knowledge and experience in sequencing changes to LTPR are critical to nation-building missions. Lastly, with a common and well-informed understanding of cadastral data, deployed U.S. civilian R&S teams could work more effectively with multi-lateral partners such as the United Nations, the North Atlantic Treaty Organization, the Organization of American States, and non-government organizations on programs for emergency humanitarian aid, for refugees, and for internally displaced persons resettlement, and infrastructure and economic recovery planning, taking into account vital LTPR issues.

The term *cadastre*, a French word of Venetian and Byzantine origins, is used deliberately. Its infrequent use in American English, coupled with its varying meanings throughout the English-speaking world and in various civil codes, serves the author's intent to define an ambiguous term and to introduce an unfamiliar concept. Among a dozen current alternatives, the International Federation of Surveyors (FIG) definition is used here.

> A *cadastre* is normally a parcel-based, up-to-date land information system containing a record of interests in land (e.g., rights, restrictions, and responsibilities). It usually includes a geometric description of land parcels linked to other records describing the nature of the interests, the ownership or control of those interests, and often the value of the parcel and its improvements.[8]

---

8 Fédération Internationale des Géomètres (FIG), The International Federation of Surveyors Commission 7, Cadastre and Land Management, *The FIG Statement on the Cadastre* (Copenhagen: The Surveyors House, 1995), URL: <*http://www.fig.net/commission7/reports/cadastre/statement_on_cadastre_summary.html*>, accessed 24 September 2007. Cited hereafter as FIG, The FIG Statement on the Cadastre.

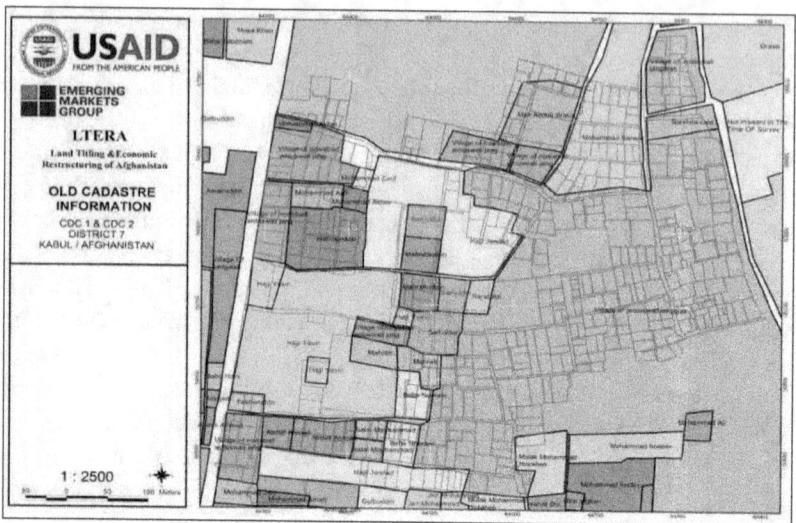

Figure 6. Old Cadastral Map of District 7, Kabul, Afghanistan. *Source: EMG.*

Cadastres have registered the human terrain for centuries. Ting and Williamson chronicled the historical relationship between land and people and the evolutionary steps in cadastral and land registration systems, which fall into four major phases:[9]

- From the age of agriculture to feudalism, human beings were physically tied to land. Land was the primary symbol and source of wealth. In this phase, the cadastre publicly recorded ownership for fiscal purposes.

- During the industrial revolution, strong physical ties to land began to dissolve and land became a conceptual, tradable commodity and the primary source of capital. This environment gave birth to land markets, and so cadastre took on another focus—a tool in land transfers.

- Post-World War II reconstruction and an increasingly mobile, growing population began to see land as a scarce resource that may not be sufficient for the world's needs. With this came growing interest in urban and regional planning, an important new application for cadastres.

- In the 1980s the earlier focus on land widened to include issues of environmental degradation, sustainable development, and social equity. All of these issues have tempered short-term economic imperatives. Planning has broadened to address community interests and detailed

---

9 Lisa Ting and Ian P. Williamson, "Cadastral Trends: A Synthesis," *The Australian Surveyor* 4, no. 1 (1999): 46-54, URL: <*http://www.sli.unimelb.edu.au/research/publications/IPW/CadastralTrendsSynthesis.html*>, accessed 25 September 2007.

land use. This growing need for more detailed information about land and land use has fueled a market for multi-purpose cadastres.

Satellite imagery has for decades been the primary way the U.S. government (USG) has answered the "where" and "what" questions, that is, how it has tracked conventional adversaries and identified their numbers and strength, for example, when it monitored Warsaw Pact T-72 tank regiments during the Cold War. Today's adversaries are not conventional armies but nameless, tenacious, and adaptive individuals who trump superior U.S. military power "by refusing to mass together and by submerging themselves in urban seas."[10]

To date the USG has invested little in collecting or creating land-related information that can answer the 'who' question, for example, who is behind poppy cultivation, ethnic cleansing, or attacks on United Nations (UN) peacekeepers. Open source and human intelligence collection has not deliberately sought to associate a personal name with a property. Narcotics traffickers, warlords, and insurgents finance their destabilizing and violent activities with wealth, wealth that often is tied to land property. Thus, analyses made with layers of cadastral data would likely increase the ability of USG policymakers to deal proactively with non-conventional foes and with world crises. An intervening military force, emergency humanitarian aid, and long-term nation-building all require an understanding of whose land interests have been affected by natural disasters or warring factions.

In its booklet, *Land and Conflict: a Toolkit for Intervention*, the U.S. Agency for International Development (USAID) aptly notes the complex relationship between land and conflict and also the crucial role of land administration in post-conflict and post-disaster reconstruction and stability.

> People have fought over land since the beginning of recorded history. Population growth and environmental stresses have exacerbated the perception of land as a dwindling resource, tightening the connection between land and violent conflict. Land is often a significant factor in widespread violence and is also a critical element in peace-building and economic reconstruction in post-conflict situations.[11]

| 5

---

10 Ralph Peters, "Out-Thought by the Enemy," *New York Post*, 1 June 2007, URL: <http://www.nypost.com/seven/06012007/postopinion/opedcolumnists/out_thought_by_the_enemy_opedcolumnists_ralph_peters.htm>, accessed 24 September 2007.

11 USAID Office of Conflict Management and Mitigation, "Land and Conflict: A Toolkit for Intervention" (Washington, DC: USAID, 2005), URL: <http://www.usaid.gov/our_work/crosscutting_programs/conflict/ publications/docs/CMM_Land_and_Conflict_Toolkit_April_2005.pdf>, accessed 24 September 2007.

The timely USAID Toolkit moves beyond a mere diagnosis of problems. It provides USG officials responding to high-profile international crises a framework to assess land-related conflict, factors to consider when developing interventions, and suggestions on how to monitor and evaluate those interventions. The Toolkit was soon followed in 2005 by the signing of National Security Presidential Directive 44 (NSPD-44), *Management of Interagency Efforts Concerning Reconstruction and Stability*. In concert with current efforts to implement NSPD-44, this book outlines the relevance of cadastral data to determine, and to achieve, desired political outcomes for post-conflict and post-disaster areas.

The book consists of eight chapters. Chapter 2 considers the relationship of land to conflict. Chapter 3 identifies the risks to stability posed by rapid urbanization and unresolved refugee plights, drawing from the refugee situation six years into Afghanistan's reconstruction. Chapter 4 makes the case that collection and analysis of cadastral data are crucial to predicting threats to regional stability, world peace, and national sovereignty expected of strategic intelligence. Chapter 5 examines the security of land tenure in the developing world and the role of cadastres in reconstructing post-conflict countries, most notably in Afghanistan. Chapter 6 presents the Land Administration Domain Model (LADM), a likely first step to an internationally recognized standard for a cadastre. The author's March 2007 research trip to Afghanistan convinced him that the LADM's flexibility for capturing both Western-style, registered land rights and the customary, informal land rights and interests typical of the developing world makes it worthy of adoption as, or to serve as a model for, a cadastral data repository. Chapter 7 identifies training in land administration as the foundation for a coordinated whole-of-government effort to address land-related crises. Chapter 8 recommends how and why cadastral and land administration expertise should be incorporated into USG R&S capabilities for a new direction in U.S. foreign policy.

CHAPTER 2:
Land and Conflict

Land conflicts appear at all geographical scales and take multiple forms. *The March*, a futuristic novel about mass migration turned into a 1990 British film, explores racial and political tensions that emerge when climate change forces millions of Africans to march en masse to the coasts of Europe. It was not for economic gain or for political asylum, but for sheer survival. In the story, a perplexed European Union Commissioner, trusted to negotiate with the march's organizer, Isa El-Mahdi, is dumbfounded when the African declares the marchers' intentions to major media outlets: "We believe that when we stand before you, you will not let us die. If you don't help us, then we will all die. You will be forced to watch how all of us die and may God be merciful to us all."[12]

In the years since the making of the film, misery on the African continent has descended to a point so abysmal as to make the novel's author, William Nicholson, wonder if he had penned fiction or not. In 1990, the United Nations Development Program (UNDP) originated the Human Development Report, also known as the *Misery Index*, to measure a nation's growth not by economic figures, but by statistical profiles of its people and what they can expect from life. In the 2000 UNDP Human Development Report, 30 of the 35 countries at the bottom of the index were sub-Saharan African nations.[13] Among the factors the index examines are the availability of schools, clean water, and medical care, and whether all citizens can play a role in politics, governance, and justice. Although these factors are related to human well-being, one major agent of social stability especially prominent in *The March* tends to be overlooked: the paramount relationship between land and people. The social-legal-economic-cultural structure of this relationship, in its variety of expressions, must be questioned, investigated, and understood.

---

12 *The March*, starring Malick Bowens and Juliet Stevenson, directed by David Wheatley, British Broadcasting Company, 1990, based on a novel by William Nicholson.

13 Barbara Crossette, "Misery Index of U.N. Panel Finds Africa Is Worst Off," *New York Times*, 5 July 2000, URL: <http://www.nytimes.com/library/world/global/070500un-africa.html>, accessed 13 June 2007.

Land is Fundamental to Human Existence

> Land is the place of all shelter, in the city, the town, the vil-
> lage, and the home. It is the source of food, of materials
> for construction and manufacture, of coal, gas and oil, of
> springs and rivers and other essentials for life. Indestructible,
> immovable, it is the foundation of all human activity. Houses
> and factories, forests and farms, river roads and railways,
> mines, quarries, and reservoirs are all fashioned from the
> land. It offers endless opportunities for development and
> discovery. It is the source of all wealth.[14]

In this speech, delivered on the eve of WWI, Sir Charles Fortescue
Brickdale, Chief Land Registrar of Great Britain, lauded the bountiful fruits
of the land secured by a century of peace in Europe. Due in no small measure
to the growth of good governance during the 19th Century, when citizens
were granted security of land tenure, Western Europe and North America
advanced from agricultural to industrial societies. The Industrial Revolution saw not only a preponderance of factories, but also the ascendancy of
classical liberalism. Noted for its defense of free economic markets and free
political thought, classical liberalism also advanced private property rights.
The principal advances in liberal land reform in the United States occurred
with the *Homestead Act* (1862) and in Canada with the *Dominion Lands Act*
(1872), both of which granted free frontier land to settlers. Those who built
on the property and lived there at least five years were promised eventual
freehold titles. Hundreds of thousands of emigrants from Europe, who never
could have dreamed of becoming landowners in the "Old Country," took
advantage of the Acts' provisions and laid the foundation for the economic
vitality of North America's heartland. The good governance responsible for
the prosperity that justified Brickdale's laudatory description of the land
resulted from secure land tenure made possible by a century of burgeon-
ing legal frameworks, democratization, industrialization, and commerce in
Western nations.

Most developing countries never experienced an industrial revolution, one of the key ingredients to the progress Brickdale hailed. Instead, the
developing world was rushed, in the 1980s and 1990s, into a neo-liberal economic market by globalization, that is, by the rapid convergence of business
practices skewed toward the patterns long established in developed coun-

---

14 Cited in United Nations Economic Commission for Europe (UNECE), Working Party on
Land Administration, *Social and Economic Benefits of Good Land Administration*," 2d ed., January
2005 (London: HM Land Registry on behalf of UNECE WPLA), 5.

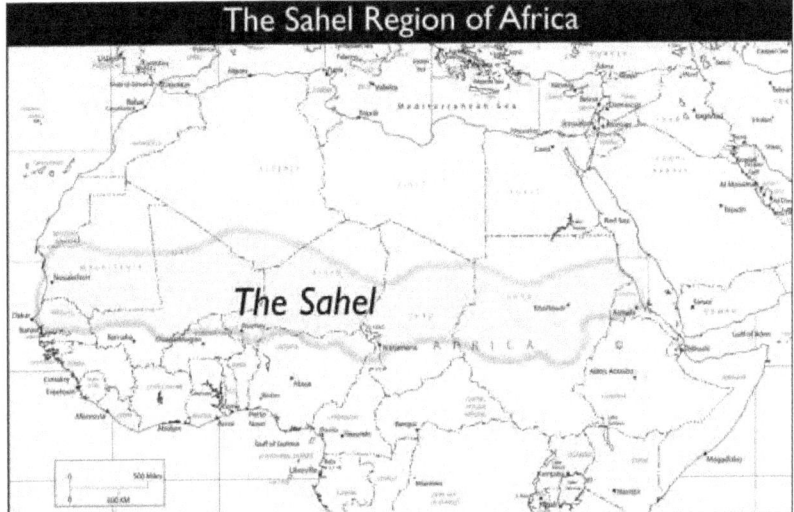

The Sahel Region of Africa

The Sahel

Figure 7. The Sahel. *Source: LTC Francis A. Galgano, A Geographical Analysis of Un-governed Spaces.*

tries. Throughout the developing world, people face grave uncertainties over, and threats to, their land: legal ambiguity, corruption, poor governance, lack of enforcement, competing claims, armed landgrabbers, and even governments bent on arbitrary eviction or expropriation of private property and land. Such threats to property rights, says Timothy Frye, can explain why underdeveloped countries remain underdeveloped, even following massive infusions of foreign aid: landless people "have little incentive to engage in productive economic behavior."[15] It has become clear in recent years that secure property rights anchor economic development. Noted economist Hernando de Soto claims that rule of law defines the relationship between land and people and that formalized property rights bring social order. Once land rights are accessible and formalized, properties can be easily conveyed, exchanged or inherited using protected, affordable, legal means. Property owners, and their countries, then prosper.

"The relationship of people to land is fundamental to human existence."[16] So begins a 2005 United Nations Economic Commission for Europe (UNECE) Working Party on Land Administration publication,

---

15 Timothy Frye, "Credible Commitment and Property Rights: Evidence from Russia," *American Political Science Review* 98, no. 3 (August 2004): 454.

16 United Nations Economic Commission for Europe, Working Party on Land Administration, *Social and Economic Benefits of Good Land Administration,*" 2d ed., January 2005 (London: HM Land Registry on behalf of UNECE WPLA), 4. Cited hereafter as UNECE WPLA, *Good Land Administration.*

which also succinctly lists 13 benefits of an effective land registration system. Such a system can[17]

- Guarantee ownership and security of tenure
- Be the basis for land and property taxation
- Provide security of credit
- Guarantee the result of judicial procedures relating to land rights, including rights of repossession of land
- Reduce land disputes
- Develop and monitor land and mortgage markets
- Protect state lands
- Facilitate land reform
- Promote improvement of land and buildings
- Facilitate reliable land use records
- Improve urban planning and infrastructure development
- Support environment management
- Produce statistical data as a base for social and economic development

From this UNECE list, it is clear that good land administration benefits all: state and local governments, the business community, and individual and family property owners.

Land Conflict Catalyzes Crises

The dissolution of the former Soviet Union markedly changed the global geo-political landscape, ushering in an era, typified by Afghanistan, where failed states pose more of a threat than does an adversarial super-power. In his 2007 Threat Assessment, the U.S. Director of National Intelligence (DNI) stated that "globalization is contributing to conflicts, instability, and reconfigurations of power and influence" and that "violent conflicts in a given state, as we see in Africa today, can swiftly lead to massive humanitarian tragedies, and potentially, regional wars."[18] While the international community is aware of the humanitarian crisis in Darfur, Karol Boudreaux, a senior research scholar at the Mercatus Center at George Mason University, points out what is less well known: "much of what underlies the con-

---

17 UNECE WPLA, *Good Land Administration*, 6.

18 John D. Negroponte, "Annual Threat Assessment of the Director of National Intelligence," report to the Senate Select Committee on Intelligence, Washington, DC, 11 January 2007, URL: <http://intelligence.senate.gov/070111/negroponte.pdf>, accessed 26 January 2007.

flicts in Darfur remain disputes over property."[19] The same can be said of the entire African continent.

> All across Africa, from the Sahel [a large swath of land at the southern fringe of the Sahara Desert] to Congo, tens of thousands of people are at war. You might think these struggles are about religion, or ethnicity, or even political differences but often you'd only be partially right. In a great many of these African struggles people are fighting their neighbors, they are not fighting because the neighbor worships God in a different way or has a different set of genes. Rather, they are fighting because this is the only way left open to them to determine who "owns" which field, or who has what rights to graze animals, or who should control the revenue from the mineral wealth below people's feet.[20]

Crises Catalyze Land Conflict

Not only do disputes over land trigger major crises; they also are effects of world crises. History is replete with examples of how wars and natural disasters have prompted large human migrations. Yet, even in the absence of armed conflict between warring groups, each year one million people are dispossessed piecemeal. This large-scale human migration, known as forced evictions, escapes media coverage and therefore Western attention. Because land is so fundamental to human existence, its loss is the ultimate catastrophe.

> Few experiences are more harrowing than being forced from one's own home. Every year many millions of people are left with no other option than fleeing their homes, lands and properties against their will. Whatever the cause, displacement is always nasty, always brutish, but all too rarely is it short. Millions of refugees and Internally Displaced Persons (IDPs) who desperately want to return to their original homes are unable to do so because restitution rights are not treated with due seriousness by relevant authorities and international actors.[21]

|11

---

19 Karol Boudreaux, "Property Holds Africa's Answer," *Enterprise Africa!* 23 September 2005, URL: <http://www.enterprise-africa.org/publications/pubid.2449/pub_detail.asp>, accessed 8 January 2007. Cited hereafter as Boudreaux, "Property Holds Africa's Answer."

20 Boudreaux, "Property Holds Africa's Answer."

21 Scott Leckie, "New Housing, Land and Property Restitution Rights," *Forced Migration Review*, no. 25 (May 2006): 52.

The Centre on Housing Rights and Evictions (COHRE) is the leading international human rights organization campaigning for the protection of housing rights and the prevention of forced evictions. The tenth edition of the COHRE Global Survey[22]—based on information received from evictees, the media, and from an expanding global network of contacts, including individuals, grassroots groups and other organizations—informally reports 4.3 million forced evictions from 2003 to 2006. The real number, currently unknown, is much higher. Over 95 percent of these evictions occurred in Africa (nearly two million) and Asia and the Pacific (over 2.1 million), an indication and warning of the nature, extent, and pervasiveness of the problem. Forced evictions, covered in the COHRE Global Survey, occur most visibly in situations of armed conflict and ethnic cleansing, or in their aftermath, but also as a result of development projects, discrimination, urban redevelopment schemes, government delineation of parklands, and so forth.

Figure 8. A Result of Violence on the Outskirts of Johannesburg, South Africa. *Source: Agence France Press.*

---

22 Centre for Housing Rights and Evictions COHRE, "Global Survey on Forced Evictions," 2007, URL: <http://www.cohre.org/view_page.php?page_id=10>, accessed 10 May 2007.

Sadly, a great number of these evictees, for whom informal, tribal, or customary property rights have for centuries secured the tenure of their homes and fields, cannot challenge the results of forced evictions when no formal, documented property records exist or these are not maintained. Once uprooted, they migrate from rural areas to cities or from city to city.

During the 1990s, the world's urban population grew by 36 percent. At the turn of the last millennium, 924 million people lived in slums, an estimated 1.4 billion will do so by 2020, and 3 billion by 2050.[23] The rapid urbanization of the world brings mounting disaffection to the slum neighborhoods.[24] "The increasing polarization of cities caused by neo-liberal globalization is providing many conditions that are ripe for extremes of civil and military violence."[25]

Anthropologist Arjun Appadurai foresees the coming urban anarchy of increased rural-to-urban migration, calling it an "implosive force that folds into neighborhoods the most violent and problematic repercussions of wider regional, national and global processes. Furthermore, displaced persons have migrated to numerous city-scale refugee camps for 50 million people worldwide, creating a new phase in the life of cities, where the concentration of ethnic populations, the availability of heavy weaponry, and the crowded conditions of civic life create futurist forms of warfare...and where a general desolation of the national and global landscape has transposed many bizarre racial, religious, and linguistic enmities into scenarios of unrelieved urban terror."[26]

An Increasing but Ineffectual International Response

In April 2006, *Refugees* magazine carried a photograph of what seems, on the surface, like a normal day at the beach. A bikini-clad woman and her bare-chested male companion sit on the sand with a cooler of cold drinks, shielded from the sun by a large umbrella. Further down the beach, another person lies on the sand, fully clothed. The third person's repose is somehow contorted, unnatural.

23 United Nations Human Settlements Programme (UN-HABITAT), *Millennium Development Goals/Overview*, 2001, URL: <http://www.unhabitat.org/content.asp?cid=2799&catid=312&typeid=24&subMenuId=0>. Cited hereafter as UN-HABITAT, *Millennium Development Goals/Overview*.

24 World Bank, *Urbanization*, 2007, URL: <http://youthink.worldbank.org/issues/urbanization/>, accessed 10 September 2007.

25 Manuel Castells, cited in *Cities, War, and Terrorism: Towards an Urban Geopolitics*, ed. Stephen Graham, ISBN 13: 978-1-4051-1575-9 (Oxford, U.K.: Blackwell Publishing, 2004), 7.

26 Arjun Appadurai, *Modernity at Large: Cultural Dimensions of Globalization*, vol. 1 of *Public Worlds Series* (Minneapolis: University of Minnesota Press, 1996), 152-153.

Goodwill Ambassador for the United Nations High Commission on Refugees (UNHCR), Angelina Jolie, in a subsequent issue of *Refugees*, laments that the couple in the photograph cannot "see the stark reality lying a few yards further up the beach. An immigrant or a refugee, sprawled across the sand...is dead. We'll never know who he was or why he ended up there, and the couple on the beach apparently couldn't care less. It is a pretty sad picture."[27]

Figure 9. The Corpse of a Would-be Migrant or Refugee on a Mediterranean Beach. *Source: Refugees Magazine, No. 142, p. 4-5 (2006), <http://www.unhcr. org/publ/PUBL/44508c182.pdf>.*

If only time would stand still, perhaps the global community could focus on one geographic region at risk or a single development issue and bring about the desired results. However, since the end of the Cold War, the accelerated dynamics of high birth rates in the developing world, rural-to-urban migrations, and globalization impede such efforts. For example, to recognize the dire circumstances of the world's urban poor in the year 2000, the UN made a Declaration on Cities and other Human Settlements in the New Millennium. Among the UN Millennium Development Goals is Target 11 Goal 7: "by 2020 to have achieved significant improvement in the lives of at least 100 million slum dwellers." Trends in population patterns suggest this worthy goal, even if it were attainable, would be neg-

---

27 Angelina Jolie, "Solving the Global Refugees Crisis," *Refugees*, October 2006, URL: <http://www.unhcr.org/publ/PUBL/4523cb392.pdf>, accessed 14 November 2006.

ligible: another UN organization estimates that the global slum-dwelling population will increase from 924 million in 2001, to 1.4 billion by 2020, and to 3 billion by 2050.[28]

The plight of the world's dispossessed have recently gained the attention of the international community. Months after the 2004 tsunami in Southeast Asia, the UN Sub-Commission on Human Rights approved a new set of "Principles on Housing and Property Restitution for Refugees and Displaced Persons," also known as the Pinheiro Principles. "The aim of the principles is to provide international standards governing one of the most basic entitlements for the survivors of a humanitarian disaster: the restitution of property."[29] Paulo Sergio Pinheiro, a UN special Rapporteur on Housing and Property Restitution, for whom the principles are named, offers his insight:

> The best solutions to the plight of millions of refugees and displaced persons around the world is to ensure that they attain the right of return freely to their countries and to have restored to them housing and property of which they were deprived during the course of displacement, or to be compensated for any property that cannot be restored to them. It is the most desired, sustainable dignified solution to displacement.[30]

The DNI's and the UN's concerns about regional instability are echoed by the International Federation of Surveyors (FIG, for Fédération Internationale des Géomètres). This non-government organization (NGO), always close to the situation on the ground, engages in land dispute resolution, in anticorruption, in transparency measures regarding land resources, and in land access for the poor. FIG-affiliated land surveyors and land administrators, chiefly from European countries, have an impressive track record of partnering with development organizations, private sector, civil society organizations, and education/research institutes to bring about sustainable development. Willi Zimmermann, an international land policy advisor with 25 years' experience with the German foreign aid organization *Gesellschaft für Technische Zusammenarbeit* (GTZ), explained at the 2006 International Federation of Surveyors (FIG) Congress:

---

28 UN-HABITAT, *Millennium Development Goals/Overview.*

29 Conor Foley and Ingunn Sofie Aursnes, "Land, Housing and Property Restitution after Conflict: Principles and Practice," *Humanitarian Exchange Magazine* (December 2005), URL: <http://www.odihpn.org/search_results.asp?page=3&searchtext=&keyword=Conflict&pubTyp e=Humanitarian+Exchange+Magazine&region=>, accessed 10 January 2007. Cited hereafter as Foley and Aursnes, "Principles and Practice."

30 Foley and Aursnes, "Principles and Practice."

Conflict prevention must be considered a global public good warranting global cooperation and action.... There is growing recognition of the threat to international security posed by failed and fragile states.... As globalization and interdependence increase, the threats posed by fragile and failed states intensify. The international community has a practical and a humanitarian responsibility to take coordinated action and to tailor specific international development efforts to halting or reversing their decline.[31]

The international community is increasingly aware of the nexus between people and land, at all scales from parcel-lots to national territory, and also between land and conflict. People and their land are so interlocked that the dissolution of that tie both causes, and is caused by, major crises. International efforts to address land issues are increasing but cannot keep pace with the problems. Unless the ruptures in, and threats to, the relationship between people and their land are addressed, the crises involving land rights and usages will overwhelm all international aid, development programs, and post-conflict reconstruction and stability efforts. As will become clear in subsequent chapters, new tools are available to meet this prodigious threat to peace and stability.

---

[31] Willi Zimmermann, "Good Governance in Land Tenure and Administration," paper TS.71-02 presented at the 23rd FIG Congress Shaping the Change, 8-13 October 2006 (Munich, Germany). Cited hereafter as Zimmermann, 2006 conference paper.

CHAPTER 3:
Land Related Crises in Afghanistan

In his March 2003 plea, "Don't Forget Afghanistan," former New York congressman and vice presidential candidate Jack Kemp recognized the significant role of land and property rights in rebuilding Afghanistan. Kemp lamented the residual power of warlords and the surge in opium cultivation that perpetuates lawlessness and finances a resurgent Taliban.

> Whatever happens in Iraq, the United States cannot afford to neglect or forget about Afghanistan. That is why we believe that a 21st century Marshall Plan for Afghanistan and the region is required, which would provide not only financial aid, but also assistance in setting up the infrastructure of democratic capitalism. And, I can think of no one better suited to advise [Afghan President] Karzai on bringing empowerment, private property and the rule of law to Afghanistan than Hernando De Soto, who has helped so many other nations, from his native Peru to Egypt, establish private property rights and leverage them as collateral for capital creation. If we can't get it right in Afghanistan, what hope will we have in Iraq?[32]

Kemp's prescient remarks about the role of property rights, made prior to the U.S.-led invasion of Iraq, deserve a closer look. His affinity for De Soto is telling. A Peruvian economist who currently runs the think tank Institute for Liberty and Democracy, De Soto is famous for championing reform in property rights and for coining the phrase "dead equity." Dead equity is the value of informally owned properties, potentially billions of dollars for many a country, locked away because such properties cannot be sold. As a principal concern, he argues that the legal processes that regulate property should be simplified and made transparent, and that formalization of property ownership can set developing countries free from their perpetual cycles of poverty, i.e., constant dissipation of any generated capital.

De Soto has won widespread praise for his work, but Kemp's affirmative endorsement of his economics is more optimistic than most experts' assessments. Nevertheless, Kemp identifies a glaring deficiency in the U.S.'s

---

32 Jack Kemp, "Don't Forget Afghanistan," *Foundation for Defense of Democracies (FDD)*, Copley News Service, 4 March 2003, URL: <http://www.defenddemocracy.org/in_the_media/in_the_media_show.htm?doc_id=160048>, accessed 11 February 2007.

development agenda for Afghanistan. Not only is Afghanistan's successful reconstruction essential for the U.S.-led Global War on Terror, but the viability and credibility of the U.S. with its multilateral, international partners, most notably the UN and North Atlantic Treaty Organization (NATO), are at stake. The lessons learned from inadequate solutions applied to the Afghan situation should alert U.S. policy makers to retool U.S. government (USG) policy and capabilities to deal effectively with the future social and economic upheavals that will fall on populations far greater than Afghanistan's estimated 32 million.[33]

Returning Afghan Refugees

From 1990 to 2006, Kelegay, Afghanistan was an empty, dusty plain; the site of an old Soviet military base with an abandoned village of broken walls cutting across untended fields. But, since 2006, frantic construction has been going on as Afghan laborers have built high-walled compounds and flat-roofed houses from mud and straw. The building boom began when the entire population of a ruined village, that had been called Naseri Chehl Kapa, came back that summer after 26 years as refugees in Pakistan. Because of their increased numbers as a new generation, they occupied government land well beyond their original village and fields, up to and over the nearby road. And, within a week, the returned villagers began dividing up the land par-

Figure 10. Afghan Walled Compounds. *Source: Dr. Gregory Maassen, EMG.*

---

[33] Central Intelligence Agency, *"The World Factbook"* (Langley, VA: Central Intelligence Agency (CIA), 2007), URL: <https://www.cia.gov/library/publications/the-world-factbook/geos/af.html>, accessed 2 July 2007.

cels and buildings. "This is our ancestral land; our forefathers lived here," said Haji Abdul Jabar, who is building a large compound that will house his family and those of his seven brothers. But, the provincial authorities say the villagers have seized the land illegally. "When these families broke the law and grabbed land, now everyone wants to grab land," complained Imamuddin Hasan, the chief Government of Afghanistan (GoA) refugee and repatriation official for Baghlan Province.

The return of Afghan refugees over the last four years, and their ability to adapt and to survive, has been one of the real successes of the international intervention and of President Hamid Karzai's government. Since the fall of

Figure 11. Afghan Refugees in Pakistan, 2001. *Source: Photo courtesy of Luke Powell, http://www.lukepowell.com.*

the Taliban in late 2001, an estimated 4.7 million refugees have flooded back from neighboring Iran and Pakistan.[34] This is a remarkable turnaround, given that a quarter of the 1980 Afghan population of 24 million fled the country.

The observations of Conor Foley, a consultant to human rights and refugee organizations, add more urgency to solving land-related refugee matters. As the story of the Kelegay returnees demonstrates, while each refugee return can be touted as a sign of success, without a land policy and a land administration system to register land rights and interests-ownership, custodianship, and use—each wave of returnees has the potential to destabilize areas once thought stable.

> Continued fighting and human rights violations mean that many other Afghans remain internally displaced, often occupying other people's lands. The looting and destruction caused by war was recently compounded by severe drought, which devastated much of the countryside over a four-year period. Disputes over land and property remain a significant cause of internal tension in Afghan society. The inability of the courts to deal with these problems is also having an extremely destabilizing effect. A recent report by the independent Afghanistan Research and Evaluation Unit described land disputes as the "number one source of conflict" in Afghanistan today.[35]

The resettlement and reintegration into society of Afghan refugees, the 4.7 million repatriated since 2002, plus the three million currently under pressure from Pakistan and Iran to return home, has become a decades-long humanitarian effort unprecedented in its scale. In addition to the millions of refugees, there are around 250,000 internally displaced persons (IDPs) in Afghanistan. Without clear definitions of who is and how long one remains an IDP, the international community's cited successes at refugee repatriation will ring hollow when "people who have fled their homes in refugee-like circumstances, but who have not crossed an international frontier receive no such aid. The practical implications of this failure continue to be felt in Afghanistan and elsewhere across the world."[36] Foley states why land ownership in Afghanistan is starkly inequitable and, consequently, a significant

---

34 Carlotta Gall, "Afghans, Returning Home, Set Off a Building Boom," *The New York Times*, 30 October 2006.

35 Conor Foley, "Afghanistan: The Search for Peace," *Minority Rights Group International*, November 2003, URL: <http://www.minorityrights.org/download.php?id=45>, accessed 23 April 2007. Cited hereafter as Conor Foley, "Afghanistan: The Search for Peace."

36 Conor Foley, "Afghanistan: The Search for Peace."

proportion of the rural population is landless, unproductive, unsheltered, and dependent.

> Returning refugees and IDPs often find themselves entangled in property disputes, are unable to reclaim their property or simply fall victim to extortion rackets run by local [militia] commanders. In the ethnically divided northern provinces in particular, where Kabul's authority holds little sway over powerful regional warlords, this is one of the most significant factors hindering return. No clear regime for managing land rights exists. The unorganized land registration system, the large number of missing title deeds, and the fact that disputed land has often been sold many times over, makes it very difficult to determine who owns what.[37]

Prior to the 2007 forced repatriations of Afghan refugees living in Iran and in Pakistan, Institute of Peace and Conflict Studies research officer Srinjoy Bose presaged that a flow of refugees back from Iran and Pakistan into Afghanistan was likely to exacerbate social and economic problems within Afghanistan. Moreover, refugees without a home or means to support themselves could join the Taliban either out of resentment or merely to survive.[38] Habibollah Qaderi, of the Afghan Ministry for Refugees and Repatriation, emphasizes that to be sustainable, refugee returns must be voluntary, informed, gradual, and linked to secure access to shelter, water, jobs, health facilities, and education. The short-term humanitarian assistance to returnees has been commendable. At a time when many NGOs in Afghanistan are tired and face dwindling donor support, long-term development programs remain pressing needs. "Good governance, respect for human rights, and the rule of law are not 'optional extras' when it comes to rebuilding a country, but an intrinsic part of the process of reconstruction."[39] The specter of three million additional Afghan refugees under pressure from Pakistan and Iran to go home bodes ill for this volatile region.

Kabul: Victim and Catalyst of Land Crises

As evidenced by the current U.S. immigration debate, millions of people are on the move and settling, legally or not, in urban and peri-urban areas of the world at an accelerating pace. Many migrants from rural areas

---

37 Conor Foley, "Afghanistan: The Search for Peace."

38 Srinjoy Bose, "Afghan Refugees in Pakistan: An Uncertain Future," *New Delhi Institute of Peace and Conflict Studies*, Report SAP20070226342002, 23 February 2007.

39 Conor Foley, "Afghanistan: The Search for Peace."

Figure 12. Informal Dwellings Built on Kabul Hillside. *Source: Dr. Gregory Maassen, EMG.*

seemingly bring only the clothes on their backs, but each also brings socio-cultural, political, and economic "baggage" to the city. "What first was invisible, when mixed into the urban cauldron of competing and antagonistic ethnicities, economies, and powers, can suddenly become incendiary in a venue laden with human tender. Indeed, urban areas are now the lightning conductors for the world's political violence."[40]

Throughout the developing world, the tremendous growth of cities, such as Lagos and Mexico City, has induced multifarious social, political, and economic troubles. Since late 2001, when the repressive Taliban regime was ousted from Afghanistan, Kabul's population has increased by 230 percent in five years, from 1.5 million to approximately 5 million, becoming one of the world's fastest growing cities.[41] Kabul's rapid urbanization, much of it informal and haphazard, has many causes: a severe drought, unemployment, fighting and insecurity, rural land disputes, and land-grabbing by the powerful. Returning refugee youth unfamiliar with agriculture but very familiar with urban life (most refugee camps have electricity, running water, and healthcare) currently flock to the cities.

---

[40] Stephen Graham, Cities, War, and Terrorism: Towards an Urban Geopolitics, ISBN 13: 978-1-4051-1575-9 (Oxford, U.K.: Blackwell Publishing, 2004), 7.

[41] USAID, Office of U.S. Foreign Disaster Assistance, "Shelter and Settlements Update: Afghanistan" (Washington, DC: USAID, October 2006). Cited hereafter as USAID, "Shelter and Settlements," 3.

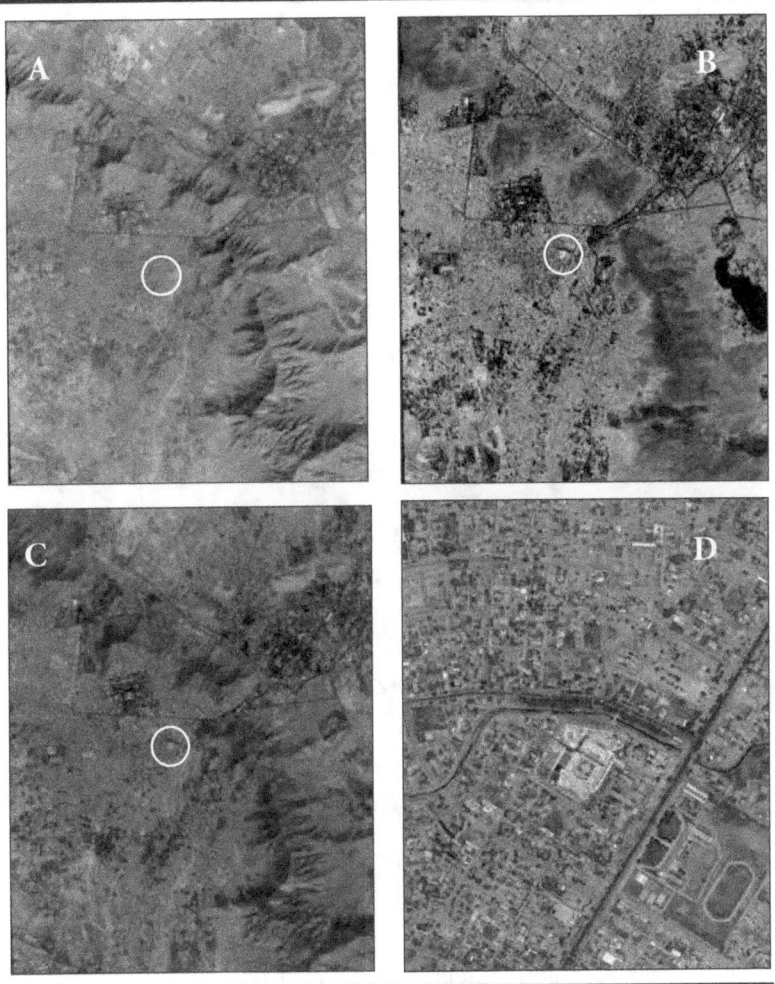

Figure 13. Change Detection Imagery of Kabul, Afghanistan. *Source: NGA Office of Science and Methodologies, Methodologies and Evaluation Division.*

    a. Landsat Enhanced Thematic Mapper-7 image from 2001

    b. QuickBird multispectral image from 2007. Downsampled to Landsat resolution. Copyright 2007 DigitialGlobe License: NextView

    c. 2001-2007 change image. Large-scale changes are visible in this image; blueish color objects are new since 2001. Note the large complex in the center.

    d. QuickBird Pan-sharpened multispectral image from 2007. Downsampled to Landsat resolution. Copyright 2007 DigitialGlobe License: NextView.

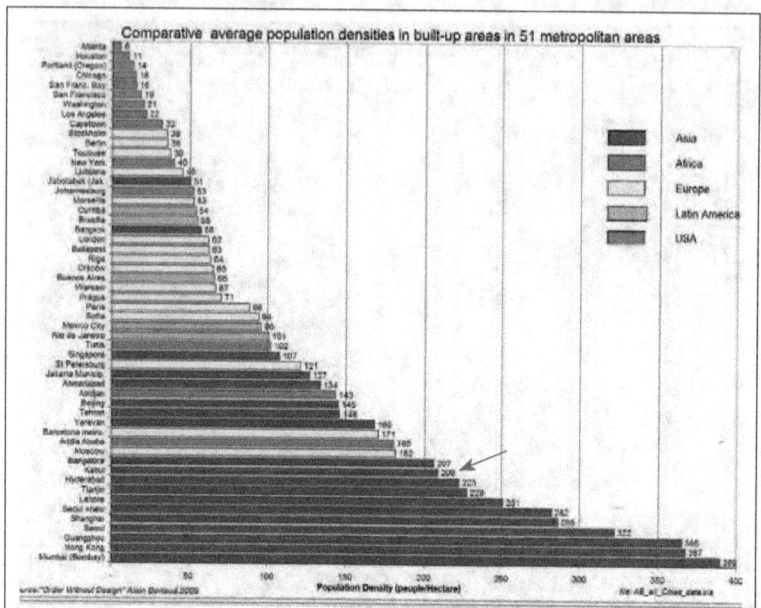

Figure 14. Comparative Average Population Densities in Built-Up Areas in 51 Metropolitan Areas Create an arrow pointing to line of the graph for Kabul. *Source: Alain Bertaud, Order Without Design, 2003. http://alain_bertaud. com/.*

During the same period, however, the physical size of Kabul, as mapped in a 1978 master plan, expanded by only 65 percent, leading to a significant increase in population density. Kabul now ranks with other South Asian megalopolises in population density, thus the accompanying inequities in land and property rights factor heavily into reconstruction and stability success. Houses in Kabul are overcrowded, with an average of 2.5 to 3 households in each single dwelling space (USAID 2006).[42]

With Kabul's population density over 200 persons per hectare (2.47 acres) or 80 persons per acre, if current trends continue, its residents will not experience many of the anticipated peace dividends. Basic indicators of human welfare place Afghans among a handful of the world's most hungry, destitute, illiterate, and short-lived people. The country ranks 173 out of 178 countries in the 2004 UNDP Human Development Index, competing with a few devastated African countries for last place. Afghan women suffer the highest rates of illiteracy and the lowest standards of health in the world.

---

42 USAID, "Shelter and Settlements," 4.

Afghanistan has the world's youngest population (an estimated 57 percent under 18 years old) and few employment prospects.[43]

Nigel Allan, Professor Emeritus of Geography at University of California-Davis, has witnessed firsthand the exponential population explosion in Afghanistan and wonders where the surplus population will go. When Allan did the field research for his dissertation in 1970, Afghanistan's population was estimated at 12 million to 14 million. He decries the current Afghan total fertility rate (TFR, the total number of children that women between the ages of 15 and 44 or 49 can expect to bear in their lifetime, given the current fertility rate) as horrific. Replacement TFR is 2.1. At this rate, a country's population remains the same. TFR for Caucasian Americans is 1.7, the same as France; for Hispanic Americans it is 2.7. In Afghanistan, the TFR is 7.48!

> Afghanistan at the moment is spewing out humans at an alarming rate and has been doing so for a number of decades because infant and child mortality has been greatly reduced by inoculation programs. While justified as a great humanitarian project, nobody ascertained what the effect of reduced mortality would be on future generations and the population/resources equation. Rural to urban migration is the norm in the less developed world. For Afghans, rural-to-urban migration is a positive force. The land cannot support the huge population-and never will.[44]

Landlessness due to poverty, land occupied by opium-cultivating warlords or squatters, land made inaccessible by mines and unexploded ordnance, clashes between Taliban militants and GoA forces, and parched land that can no longer sustain livelihoods are reasons why returnees have settled in Kabul's slums rather than their ancestral homes. Inexorably drawn to Kabul in search of job security and social cohesion, returnees without security of land tenure in their former pastoral lands find their new existence in informal urban slums equally untenable for an equivalent reason. Nevertheless, they stay.

Among other impediments, land tenure insecurity threatens to undermine the achievements of post-conflict, stabilized Afghanistan, such as

---

43 USAID, "Shelter and Settlements," 4.

43 Barnett R. Rubin and Humayun Hamidzada, "From Bonn to London: Governance Challenges and the Future of Statebuilding in Afghanistan," *International Peacekeeping* 14, no. 1 (February 2007):20.

44 Nigel J.R. Allan, USA, Professor of Geography Emeritus, University of California at Davis, e-mail interview by the author, 16 May 2007.

Figure 15. The Author Chats with Youths in Herat. Fifty-seven Per Cent of Afghans Are Under Age 18. *Source: Author.*

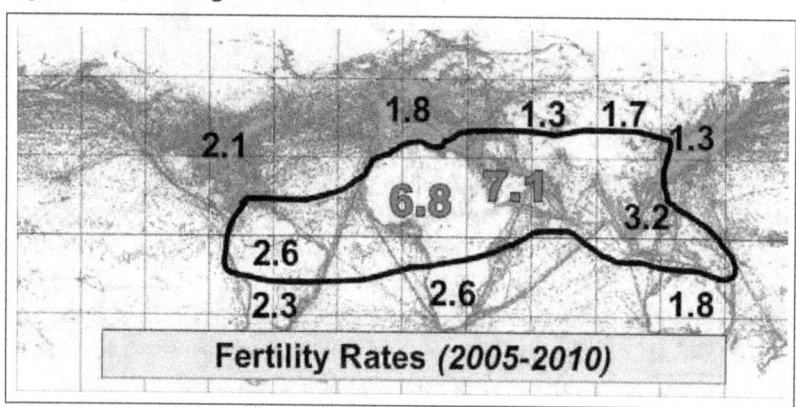

Figure 16. Regional Total Fertility Rates (TFR). An evident, inverse correlation exists between affluence and a lower fertility rate, as reflected by the location of dense lines of communication (in red) and corresponding TFRs. *Source: Office of the Chief of Navy Reserve, http://navyreserve.navy.mil.*

a legitimately elected president, a progressive national constitution, a free press, and a host of new schools. No doubt improvements have been made, but they are dwarfed by the increased demand for essential services and infrastructure in the rapidly growing cities, Kabul especially. The invisibility of anxiously awaited improvements heightens the disparities between the haves and the have-nots. Rubin notes:

17. Gasoline for Sale for Use in Private Generators. *Source: Dr. Gregory Maassen, EMG.*

A major economic issue that is aggravating relations between Afghans and the international community is the supply of electricity to Kabul. As the city's population expands toward five million (up from 2.3 million in 2001), Kabulites today have less electricity than they did five years ago. While foreigners and the rich power air conditioners, hot water heaters, high-speed internet, and satellite TV with private generators, average Kabulites are now ending a summer without fans, and fearing a winter without heaters.[45]

The Conditions of Land Crises in Afghanistan at a Glance

In 2006, the Geographic Research Branch of the U.K. Defence Geographic Centre summarized how decades of chaos have affected the relationship of people to land in Afghanistan.[46]

- The present legislation on land tenure in Afghanistan is complex, uncertain and incomplete. Land relations in Afghanistan have been

---

45 Barnett R. Rubin, "Still Ours to Lose: Afghanistan on the Brink," written testimony, Senate Foreign Relations Committee, Washington, DC, 21 September 2006, 7. Cited hereafter as Rubin, "Still Ours to Lose: Afghanistan on the Brink."

46 U.K. Defence Geographic Centre, Geographic Research Branch, "Summary of Land Ownership in Afghanistan," (Middlesex, U.K.: October 2006).

governed by a number of legal frameworks, and these frameworks have been interpreted differently by successive administrations; therefore, identifying the current law is a challenge.

- Stark inequalities in land ownership, ethnic conflict over land access, and mismanaged land reforms by the state have generated and sustained conflict over the past 25 years.
- No clear regime for managing land rights exists and, by default, many management functions have fallen to the courts, which handle the bulk of land disputes. With instability and coercion by warlords over the last decade, land rights management and dispute resolution lost credibility in many areas.
- Most rural Afghans regulate their land ownership relations customarily, without using officials or courts. Customary sector management offers a strong foundation, but is rife with practices that favor wealthier elites, men, and dominant ethnic groups.
- The rules addressing who may own land in Afghanistan and in what circumstances vary depending on the type of land under consideration.

Foley, likewise, captures both the chaotic nature of land conflict in Afghanistan and how the absence of rule of law and civil institutions are impediments to sustainable development:[47]

- Houses have often been destroyed or occupied by others, and these "secondary occupants" may themselves have been driven from their homes.
- Official records proving ownership may have been destroyed, or were never entirely accurate to begin with.
- Ownership and transfer documents are often forged.
- People may have been compelled to "sell" their land or property under duress.
- People who have lived in a particular place for years may not have an official title, because it was in the form of social ownership or only recognized through customary law.

28 | Priorities for Addressing Afghanistan's Land Crises

The challenge is daunting and of a higher order. Similar to the lower levels of human needs in Maslow's hierarchy, lower level nation-building needs must be addressed to bolster progress on higher levels. The authors of *The Beginner's Guide to Nation-Building* emphasize that the first-order pri-

---

47 Conor Foley, *A Guide to Property Law in Afghanistan*, 1st ed. (Oslo/Pakistan/Afghanistan: Norwegian Refugee Council (Flyktninghjelpen), 2005), 204.

orities for any nation-building mission are public security and humanitarian assistance. They propose the following priority of nation-building tasks, starting with the most urgent:[48]

1. *Security*: peacekeeping, law enforcement, rule of law, and security sector reform

2. *Humanitarian Relief:* return of refugees and response to potential epidemics, hunger, and lack of shelter

3. *Governance:* resuming public services and restoring public administration

4. *Economic Stabilization:* establishing a stable currency and providing a legal and regulatory framework in which local and international commerce can resume

5. *Democratization:* building political parties, free press, civil society, and a legal and constitutional framework for elections

6. *Development:* fostering economic growth, poverty reduction, and infrastructure improvements

The above activities need not be accomplished sequentially. If adequate funding is available, they can and should proceed in tandem. But if more urgent priorities are not adequately resourced, investment in less urgent (but no less important) ones is likely to be wasted.[49]

Addressing the deteriorating situation in Afghanistan, President Bush asked Congress for $10.6 billion in more aid for Afghanistan for 2007, primarily to increase security. A quarter of this aid, a good $2.6 billion, will go largely to building an electrical power distribution system—only 6 percent of Afghans now have dependable electrical power—and to constructing roads.[50] The bulk of the 2007 aid package attends to the more urgent needs while at the same time recognizing that long-term economic development requires a legitimate, non-narcotics-based economy and land tenure security based on the rule of law. In parallel, a corruption-free public administration in the form of credible and efficient institutions will have to manage the resettlement of returned refugees. Hence, the difficulties of the people-land

---

48 James Dobbins, Seth G. Jones, Keith Crane, Beth Cole DeGrasse, *The Beginner's Guide to Nation-Building*, ISBN 978-0-8330-3988-0 (Arlington, VA: RAND Corporation, 2007), xxiii. Cited hereafter as Dobbins, Jones, Crane and DeGrasse, The Beginner's Guide to Nation-Building.

49 Dobbins, Jones, Crane and DeGrasse, *The Beginner's Guide to Nation-Building.*

50 Elaine Shannon, "Can More Aid Save Afghanistan?" Time, 26 January 2007, URL: <http://www.time.com/time/printout/0.8816.1582650.99.html>, accessed 18 April 2007.

Figure 18. A Provincial Reconstruction Team (PRT). *Source: U.S. Department of Defense.*

relationship are intertwined at all stages: from registering the familial parcel lot to controlling State lands and cross-border activities. Even abroad, the botched diplomacy with Iran over reception of the tens of thousands of deported Afghans nearly resulted in the sacking of Afghan Foreign Minister Rangin Dadfar Spanta in June 2007. Thus, the linchpin for the success of all foreign aid projects in Afghanistan is law and order.

Afghanistan expert Barnett R. Rubin foresees a multi-year, perhaps decades-long, transition from customary law to civil and state law. Keenly aware that a lack of law enforcement undermines the basic legitimacy of any government, Rubin, from his 2006 travels in the country, recognizes that "the only capacities for dispute resolution and law enforcement that actually exist in much of Afghanistan consist of informal or village councils or mullahs who administer a crude interpretation of sharia. Community leaders complained constantly about judicial corruption. Many demanded the implementation of sharia law, which they contrast not to secular law, but to corruption. During the years required for [judicial reform] the only genuine alternatives before Afghan society will be the enforcement of such customary or Islamic law, or no law."[51] The avowal of community decisions and initiatives is in concert with Jalali and Grau's assertion that if Afghanistan is to

---

[51] Rubin, "Still Ours to Lose: Afghanistan on the Brink," 10.

regain stability, the fractured social order must be restored by the empowerment of civil (tribal, community) leaders.[52]

De Soto's Proposal: A Viable Solution?

As Afghan and foreign experts address land tenure matters, they will be looking for a remedy to Afghanistan's broader problems. Consider Kemp's hearty endorsement of Hernando De Soto's poverty alleviation strategies. Would De Soto's advocacy of land reform—amending laws currently at odds with local customs of understanding and dealing in land, and re-inventing land registration systems that are not within reach or useful to the vast majority of a country's citizens—work in Afghanistan? Although De Soto has won wide acclaim for his work, most notably from former President Bill Clinton, he has been criticized for offering a silver-bullet solution to poor countries' complex tribulations. In the case of Afghanistan, this caution is commendable because a single solution may not fit its myriad land tenure issues. The application of his principles in different parts of the world have yielded uneven results. In some countries, De Soto-like ideals play out beautifully and bring about prosperity; in other places, his reforms are ineffectual or even destabilizing. Ben Cousins and Donna Hornby detail difficulties in South Africa's experiment with reforms advocated by De Soto:

> Renowned economist Hernando De Soto says he has found an answer to global poverty. "Let's give poor people individual titles to the land so they can access credit, loans, and investment, and transform it into live capital," he once said. Powerful words by an expert whose ideas have been packaged and peddled all over the developing world by international development agencies. In South Africa, where land ownership is a controversial issue, the notion of providing individual title to land previously owned through customary or collective land rights has become fashionable in development circles. This approach, trumpeted by De Soto, is intended to "capitalize the poor," as in the West where every piece of land is documented as part of a vast legal process that endows owners with the potential to use it as collateral or capital. Land titling in South Africa has engendered strong opposition from NGOs, social movements, and some land rights experts. Why aren't they celebrating

| 31

52 Ali Ahmad Jalali and Lester W. Grau, Department of the Army, "Putting Humpty Dumpty Together Again" (Fort Leavenworth, Kansas, Foreign Military Studies Office, December 2001), 1.

De Soto's prescriptions? Because his policy prescriptions oversimplify the complexities of informal economy and land rights... This approach can actually weaken land rights and marginalize vulnerable people.[53]

A boon to some, perilous to others: the truth about the value of individual land titling in developing countries lies somewhere in between. A study conducted in Argentina determined that individual land titles can have positive effects, even if the prosperity De Soto envisions is not an immediate result. Galiani and Schargrodsky, of the Stanford University Center for International Development, found a modest but positive effect of land titling on access to mortgage credit, but no impact on access to other forms of credit. Yet, "moving a poor household from *usufructuary* land rights to full property rights substantially increased investment in the houses."[54] Moreover, land titling reduced the fertility of the household heads, and the presence of extended family members. Also, these smaller families invested more resources in the education of their children.

In sum, "entitling the poor increases their investment both in the house and in the human capital of their children, which will contribute to reduce the poverty of the next generation."[55] While secondary and tertiary effects from individual land titling, such as smaller, better educated families, may disappoint De Soto devotees, such results would be welcome in Afghanistan, a nation struggling to emerge from decades of conflict and devastation.

The Housing, Land, and Property Rights Triad

The year 2007 marks the first time in human history that the number of city dwellers surpassed the world's rural population. In Afghanistan, the capital city, Kabul, the destination of millions of repatriated refugees and IDPs, is the most visible urban area in the developing world grappling with rural-to-urban migration. Hard-pressed to absorb these numbers, much less any of the remaining three million refugees who face an uncertain future in neighboring countries, Afghanistan is the 21st century proving ground for approaches to reconstruction and stability. De Soto's reforms may certainly constitute part of the solution to Afghanistan's land crises and community needs. But his larger theories must yield, when necessary, to those culturally

53 Ben Cousins and Donna Hornby, "Land Rights: De Soto Solution Not for South Africa," *Business Day*, 13 January 2007, 1.

54 Sebastian Galiani and Ernesto Schargrodsky, *Property Rights for the Poor*, Working Paper #249 (Palo Alto, CA: Stanford University Center for International Development, 2005): 30. Cited hereafter as Galiani and Schargrodsky, "Property Rights for the Poor."

55 Galiani and Schargrodsky, *Property Rights for the Poor*, 30.

attuned applications that can best build a civil society and a legitimate economy, anchors for sustainable development in Afghanistan. Foley elaborates, "The issue of housing, land, and property (HLP) rights should be considered as one central, but interlinked component of a process of nation-building. Perhaps a central lesson from Afghanistan is that a 'one size fits all' approach to HLP is rarely likely to be successful at the national level. It is essential, instead, that those involved in designing and implementing HLP rights programs have a clear understanding of the cultural, social, and political context in which they are working."[56]

Even though land issues do not have the urgency that other short-term humanitarian crises do, resolving land conflicts can address both long-term and short-term needs and can foster stability in Afghanistan. In the remaining chapters, it will become apparent that lack of a land administration system that registers multiple (shared or even competing) rights and interests in land—as opposed to private property rights—may be the deciding factor between success and failure for the international community's six-year investment in Afghanistan.

---

56 Conor Foley, *Housing, Land and Property Restitution Rights in Afghanistan* (Centre for Housing Rights and Evictions COHRE, in press 2006), 31, URL: <http://www.cohre.org>, accessed 5 April 2007. Cited hereafter as Foley, *Housing, Land and Property Restitution Rights*.

CHAPTER 4:
"Foreign Intelligence is Geography"

— *Jerome Dobson*

Recent U.S. Intelligence Failures

Numerous books, all critical, most scathing, some commiserating, but few perceptive, have appeared in recent years to bemoan a litany of post Cold-War U.S. intelligence failures, diplomatic blunders, alienated allies and enraged adversaries. The terror attacks of September 11, 2001, prompted a mammoth reorganization and consolidation of 22 separate agencies into the U.S. Department of Homeland Security in 2003. The 16 agencies composing the IC, since 2005 under a single Director of National Intelligence, now collaborate on the basis of "responsibility to provide" as opposed to the previous "need to know." And technological advances such as the Wiki-inspired Intellipedia allow analysts to add personal insights to an ever-increasing aggregate of information. Years before the September 11th attacks, and days before the East African Embassy bombings that foreshadowed them, John Hillen cited unfamiliarity with the Kosovo Liberation Army and total stupefaction at Indian nuclear tests as evidence that the Intelligence Community (IC) was replete with information-saturated Know Nothings.[57] U.S. intelligence assets were, and still are, too skewed toward technical solutions to decipher the cultural currents of foreign shores.

A decade ago Hillen wrote that "the U.S. is unusually clueless on things it really must know, such as what stands to happen in post-Suharto Indonesia, the security of Russia's nuclear weapons (and scientists), China's intentions about virtually anything outside its borders, Japan's economic and trading strategies, or the state of the North Korean regime."[58] Dobson reflects on the Iraq "quagmire," noting that U.S. "policy makers did not take culture—Shia Arab, Sunni Arab, and Sunni Kurd—adequately into account in post-war planning for

---

[57] John Hillen, "Know Nothings: U.S. Intelligence Failures Stem from Too Much Information, Not Enough Understanding," *National Review* 50, no. 14 (3 August 1998): 1. Cited hereafter as Hillen, "Know Nothings."

[58] Hillen, "Know Nothings," 2.

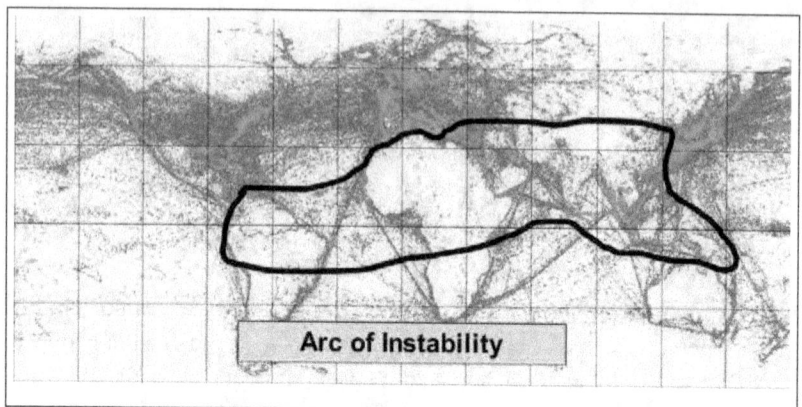

Figure 19. The Arc of Instability Encompasses the Least Affluent Regions of the World. *Source: Office of the Chief of Navy Reserve, http://navyreserve.navy.mil.*

Iraq."[59] Iraq is but an example of how "the United States is now a mighty global power crippled by abysmal ignorance of its vast global domain."[60]

A list of geopolitical concerns for 2007 might be headlined by a post-Musharraf Pakistan, Iran's nuclear capabilities and intentions, Hizbollah's de facto state-within-a-state influence in Lebanon, China's economic investments in Panama and Africa, and the consequences of a unilateral declaration of Kosovar independence. And those are concerns in the governed regions of the world. Thinking geographically about the large, porous, ungoverned regions, devoid of political control, presents a greater challenge still. The western provinces in Pakistan, portions of Lebanon and Yemen, wide swaths of South America (Amazonia) and Africa, the Sahel and the Horn, parts of the southern Philippines, several Indonesian islands, Chechnya, and rural Myanmar are outside effective government control and thus can be affected severely by humanitarian disasters and ethnic conflict. "These regions are defined by endemic imbalances in the distribution of wealth, staggering health problems, fragile political systems, regressive social systems and disenfranchised youth susceptible to the lure of extremism. They contain equal potential for either positive growth, or catastrophic failure,"[61] which is why they should be of particular concern to the IC.

---

59 Jerome E. Dobson, "Foreign Intelligence Is Geography," *Ubique — Notes from the American Geographical Society (AGS)* 25, no. 1 (2005): 1-2. Cited hereafter as Dobson, "Intelligence is Geography."

60 Dobson, "Intelligence is Geography."

61 Francis A. Galgano, "A Geographical Analysis of Un-Governed Spaces," *The Pennsylvania Geographer* 44, no. 2 (Fall/Winter 2006): 72.

Geography in 20th Century U.S. Foreign Policy and Academe

Dobson recalls the first half of the 20th century as a time when the forging of American foreign policy could not have been accomplished without geographers. In the aftermath of the "War to End all Wars, U.S. President Woodrow Wilson believed that America would lead the world in peace through political and economic, rather than military means. Wilson called on a distinguished geographer, the Harvard and Yale educated Isaiah Bowman, to help frame American foreign policy at the 1919 Paris Peace Conference.

Figure 20. Isaiah Bowman.
Source: American Geographical Society.

Wilson's plight is especially instructive. For 140 years, America had practiced isolationism. No one in government—not even the officers and analysts of the Department of State or Military Intelligence—was ready to analyze foreign intelligence or face sophisticated European negotiators. Wilson, scholar that he was, recognized his problem as being geographic and called on the AGS for help. AGS director Bowman led *The Inquiry*, a massive analysis of foreign intelligence staffed by 150 scholars from geography and other disciplines. Their task was to collect and analyze the information that would be needed to establish a "scientific" peace at war's end. As part of The Inquiry, the AGS was responsible for drafting Wilson's famous Fourteen Points, one of the most reassuring and effective policy statements ever written. When Wilson and the American delegation left for France, Bowman sailed with them. On arrival, Bowman pulled off an amazing bureaucratic coup, and Wilson decreed that analysts from the Department of State, Military Intelligence, and Central Bureau of Statistics would report to him through Bowman. In January 1919, AGS geographers and cartographers turned out more than 300 maps per week based on geographic analysis of The Inquiry's massive data collections covering language, ethnicity, resources, historic boundaries, and other pertinent information. America's delegation became the envy of Versailles.[62]

62 Jerome E. Dobson, "Bring Back Geography!" *ArcNews Online by ESRI*, Spring 2007, URL:<http://www.esri.com/news/arcnews/spring07articles/bring-back-geography-1of2.html>, accessed 18 July 2007. Cited hereafter as Dobson, "Bring Back Geography!"

One might think that the American political isolationism at the time would have found geographers, especially political geographers with expertise on foreign areas, wanting. That was hardly the case. The focus of geography until about 1850 was celestial navigation. Charles Darwin's theories of evolution revolutionized geography; the discipline increasingly catechized the relationship between land and people. By the turn of the 20th century, the "Heyday of Ivy League Geography,"[63] America's first professional geographers, like their European counterparts, held fast to the prevailing theory of environmental determinism. Simply stated, environmental determinism postulates that physical geography, including climate, at a minimum influences people or, according to some, even determines mentalities and cultures. Tropical climates dispose inhabitants toward sloth, for example, while the harsher weather of the middle latitudes leads to perseverance, and to social and industrial progress. The theory's Darwinian "survival of the fittest" tenet is obvious.

The environmental deterministic works of Friedrich Ratzel, a German geographer who invented the term "*Lebensraum*" ("room for living"), were influential in stoking the arms race of Imperial Germany. Ratzel's 1875 tour of the American Midwest acquainted him with the positive influence German immigrants had had as a fertilizing element on the culture of the newly settled frontier. The aggressive, "*Übermensch*" or superior man ideology of Nazi Germany came not from Ratzel, but from Karl Haushofer and his *Geopolitik* or German geostrategy. Haushofer, a former military attaché to Japan and a WWI general, became a geography professor at the University of Munich, where future Deputy *Reichsführer* Rudolf Hess was his student. As founding editor of the *Zeitschrift für Geopolitik*, the "Magazine of Geopolitics," he so influenced geographers in Japan that a school of geopolitics modeled after Haushofer's was established there. Haushofer helped craft the WWII German-Japanese alliance; he committed suicide in 1946. The environmental determinism that charged *Geopolitik* became the bedrock, first of Adolf Hitler's bellicose speeches, and later of his horrific foreign policy. Haushofer proffered a scientific justification of *Geopolitik*:

> As an exact science, *Geopolitik* deserves serious consideration. Our leaders must learn to use all available tools to carry on the fight for Germany's existence—a struggle which is becoming increasingly difficult due to the incongruity between her food production and population density . . . Germany must emerge out of the narrowness of her present

---

63 Richard Wright and Natalie Koch, *Geography in the Ivy League* (Hanover, NH: Dartmouth College, in press 2007), 5, URL: <http://www.dartmouth.edu/~geog/dc_geo_AG_WGl1.html>, accessed 15 July 2007. Cited hereafter as Wright and Koch, *Geography in the Ivy League.*

living space into the freedom of the world....We must familiarize ourselves with the important spaces of settlement and migration on Earth. We must study the problem of boundaries as one of the most important problems of *Geopolitik*. We ought to devote particular attention to national self-determination, population pressure, living space.[64]

In later life Bowman's views, especially as a co-architect of the UN, exhibited probabilistic, as opposed to deterministic, geographical thought. The European Union, adding ever more member states, is a half-century testimonial for regional cooperation among naturally competitive polities. Nevertheless, immediately after German capitulation in 1945, *Geopolitik* fell into disrepute as a bizarre Nazi pseudoscience responsible for 70 million deaths. Academia quickly distanced itself from environmental determinism, the theory behind *Geopolitik*, and, in the U.S., quite inexplicably, associated geography as a whole with Nazism. Lacking alternative operable theories to environmental determinism, scholars then berated geography for being poorly defined, and for its best work having been done by non-geographers.[65] Dartmouth College geography professor Richard Wright and Harvard University graduate student Natalie Koch explain a trend that began in 1948 when Harvard, soon followed by Stanford, Yale and other leading universities, closed its geography departments.

The reasons behind these terminations vary around themes of weak faculty and the discipline's uncertain intellectual terrain. The adverse fiscal context faced by institutions in the aftermath of World War II probably made things worse. Increased demand for practical education and the attack on environmental determinism was particularly devastating for the future of geography in the Ivy League universities, which increasingly emphasized the importance of theory and held technical instruction in low esteem. In contrast, geography departments in the land-grant colleges of the Midwest prospered in this environment. Because these universities were designed in part to support the Midwestern agricultural economy and serve the broader public, they welcomed the applied elements of geography.[66]

---

64 Andreas Dorpalen, *The World of Haushofer: Geopolitics in Action* (New York: Farrar & Rhinehart, Inc., 1942), 28.

65 Wright and Koch, *Geography in the Ivy League*, 8.

66 Wright and Koch, *Geography in the Ivy League*, 7.

The Ivy League geography departments closed in favor of new area studies and political science curriculums. These newer disciplines often lack a spatial component. Widespread disdain for geography as an applied, rather than a basic, science saw geography replaced in many universities by urban planning, which is far more applied, pragmatic, and arguably vocational. Noting these contradictions, Dobson, incredulous that any discipline could be so drastically punished for its alleged shortcomings, acclaims geography as much more than its recent consignment to leisure travel and photo journals popularized by *National Geographic*:

> Geography is more than you think! Geography is to space what history is to time. It is a spatial way of thinking, a science with distinctive methods and tools, a body of knowledge about places, and a set of information technologies that have been around for centuries. Geography is about understanding people and places and how real-world places function in a viscerally organic sense. It's about understanding spatial distributions and interpreting what they mean. It's about using technology to study, in the words of the late professor J. Rowland Illick, "why people do what they do where they do it." Geography is a dimensional science, based on spatial logic in which locations, flows, and spatial associations are considered to be primary evidence of earth processes, both physical and cultural. Its hallmarks are spatial analysis, place-based research (e.g., regional, area, and urban studies) and scientific integration.[67]

Recovering Geography in the 21st Century

Fifty years ago the launch of the Sputnik satellite caused widespread alarm but also presented a tangible objective for American foreign policy. The adversarial Soviets had seemingly surpassed the U.S. in rocket and, by implication, missile technology. To recover from the shock and embarrassment, Congress, passing the National Defense Education Act, infused federal money into K-12 teacher education and built a pipeline leading students from phonics to university degrees in math and science. In 1969 the U.S. won the space race against the Soviets to put a man on the moon.

The challenges facing the U.S. in the 21st century as the world's sole super power are less technical but immensely more complex. Not only because human behavior is complex, but because yet another dimension to the battlespace has

---

67 Dobson, "Bring Back Geography!"

appeared, the third new realm to be contested in under a century. From time primordial to WWI, the battlespace was limited to the earth's surface—land and sea. "Control of the skies" or airpower proved to be decisive in the Allied victory in WWII. In the late 20th century, from Sputnik to the Strategic Defense Initiative "Star Wars," the battlefield expanded into a third dimension—space. The Global War on Terror once again catches the U.S. behind its adversaries in operating in a fourth dimension, virtual space, not only in exercising effective command and control, but in promulgating ideologies. Vitriolic virtual media coverage of U.S. foreign policy missteps has cemented anti-American sentiment in many corners of the world. The lack of a galvanized U.S. assertion of its positive international identity, one that might equate to Franklin's Roosevelt's casting of America as an "arsenal of democracy" in 1940, allows the extremist ideologies to go unchallenged and worse, to be operationalized. Are further U.S. foreign policy embarrassments necessary to recover an understanding of "why people do what they do where they do it?"

In a century of transitions in warfare the real world has not been so easy to see as the theoretical. Wars on the surface still go on. Conflicts in air and space continue. The venues of virtual warfare are so new that those on the defensive have been slow to respond if not completely overwhelmed. The capabilities afforded by new technologies have been difficult to absorb and use to an advantage, altering the very concept of what is national security.

The increasing affordability of the Internet and other virtual technologies has greatly increased communications in the developing world. Cellular phone provider Vodaphone recently took over half of the telephone system for the Republic of the Congo and offered monthly service for as low as $2 per user. Now a street vendor making $8 a day can afford a telephone. Similarly, other technologies have dramatically dropped in price, making their use feasible in areas without electricity. Another example now available worldwide is the global positioning system (GPS). In affluent countries, drivers have been thrilled to see prices of these systems drop from thousands of dollars to $300 in less than a decade, all the while with improved real-time traffic reports and voice commands. Simpler GPSs, but with laser pointers and surveying capability, are available to users at prices that make them viable to employ even by the poorer states.

Using inexpensive GPS surveying tools, governments and individuals can produce cadastral maps that tell residents, farmers, shop owners, and others exactly where their properties are in relation to goods and services, markets, and transportation nodes. Using Geographic Information Science (GIS) they can even record details as to the uses of the land and the various details of it—geology, drainage, crops, soils, economic use, affiliation of the owner, and other variables. This openly available, but often unrecorded, information is the basis not only of business intelligence decisions, but of peoples' ways of life. GIS allows better understanding of a culture, its customs and norms regarding land use, property ownership, and the development of the local infrastructure.

Attorney and former U.S. military attaché officer Geoffrey Demarest contends that foreign policy decisions, whether related to counter-narcotics, counter-terrorism, economic aid, nation-building, and so on, are ill-founded when not informed by intelligence regarding the ownership of real property. Moreover, the link between the existence of formalized property and internal peace is direct and substantial. The implication for the Intelligence Community (IC) is compelling. In addition to economic, political, and military intelligence, the IC must expand its product line to include property intelligence.[68]

Foreign Intelligence is Geography. As taught in university-level regional geography courses, open-source geography offers an untapped intelligence bonanza. Once transformed into property intelligence, open-source geography, such as property information, can potentially predict the course of civil violence, determine the effectiveness of an opium eradication campaign, and uncover heretofore hidden familial, financial, and organizational ties of non-state actors, the murky adversaries in the Global War on Terror.

> After all, the scale of danger presented by an individual or organization is somehow commensurate with their material wealth....The leaders of the Colombian FARC or of Al Qaeda manage considerable wealth and defend territory by secrecy and force. If secrecy of ownership were unavailable to them, and their wealth and sanctuaries exposed, then their ability to use violent force would be insufficient to keep them from losing power. Such leaders are well aware of this fact....They are careful to protect the lack of records and confidentiality of the wealth that the lack of a formalized property system assigns to them. Not only can we take their wealth away, it will lead us to them. It is their Achilles heel.[69]

Demarest adds that property, as a subject of study, provides a link between law and geography. U.S. intelligence collectors, analysts, and policy makers, historically indifferent to details of property ownership, with new GIS applications can exploit property ownership data to refine national intelligence

---

68 Geoffrey Demarest, *Property & Peace: Insurgency, Strategy and the Statute of Frauds*, report for the U.S. Army, Foreign Military Studies Office (Ft. Leavenworth, KS: Foreign Military Studies Office, 2007), 80. Cited hereafter as Demarest, *Property & Peace.*

69 Demarest, *Property & Peace,* 53.

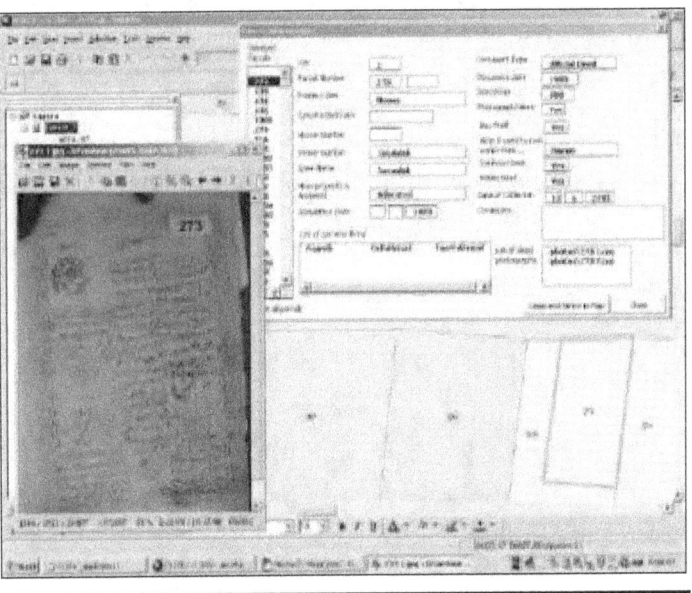

Figure 21. Old Cadastral Records Overlaid onto Commercial Satellite Image of Current Parcel Boundaries, and Figure 22. A Matching Property Deed—Tying a Name to a Place. *Source: EMG.*

strategy. "We should recover geography itself as a discipline for matters of state, because the object of ownership, and of most armed struggles is, after all, a place. It is simultaneously the link between economics and strategy, assessing and addressing internal conflicts, allowing precise assignment of relative value to territory."[70]

Foley, prescribing remedies for the international community to untangle the 40-year impact that tribalism, communism, Islamic theocracy, and now the lure of a free market economy has successively had on land and property in Afghanistan, rightly concludes, "send money, guns, and lawyers."[71] The U.S. is sending money and guns to Afghanistan and elsewhere, but very little in the way of legal, social, and land administration experts because such deployable expertise resides neither in the ranks of USG foreign aid workers nor in universities that prepare students for foreign service and international development careers. Although the U.S. is afflicted by a dearth of foreign geographic knowledge, there are signs of change, beginning with the military forces. Dobson, in one-on-one conversations with General David H. Petraeus, commander of the Multi-National Force-Iraq (MNF-I), has sufficient reason for optimism that geography's indispensable role in war and peace will not be relegated to the past. General Petraeus "holds a doctorate in international relations from Princeton University's Woodrow Wilson School of Public and International Affairs, and he's every bit as smart as you've heard. His innate sense of geography comes through in his 14 observations from soldiering in Iraq. Observation number nine says, 'Cultural awareness is a force multiplier,' and he adds, 'knowledge of the cultural 'terrain' can be as important as, and sometimes even more important than, knowledge of the geographic terrain.'"[72] Dobson's interaction with General Petraeus indicates that influential leaders can modify their impressions of geography.

70 Demarest, Property & Peace, 9.
71 Foley, Housing, Land and Property Restitution Rights, 30.
73 Dobson, "Bring Back Geography!"

New Geographical Tools and Applications

Geographic Information System

Intelligence Preparation of the Environment is the graphical analysis of the enemy, environment, and terrain for all types of military operations. GIS is the civilian counterpart, a visual depiction of a given problem's geospatial components such as transportation networks, income distribution, demographic factors, land use, and property ownership. GIS has created a body of actionable knowledge far greater in size than open-source textual data, but until the maturing of GIS, around the turn of the millennium, an assertion that property intelligence could inform policy makers as well as economic, political, and military intelligence, would have been viewed as fanciful. Michael F. Goodchild, Professor of Geography at the University of California, Santa Barbara, describes GIS as "a way of looking at the world, a lens through which the world is filtered as it is projected on the geographer's screen...and access to a vast range of analytic techniques that can test theories and hypotheses or search for patterns and anomalies."[73] With the advent of MapQuest and Zillow, GIS applications for navigation and real estate valuations, respectively, it is no longer a pipe dream

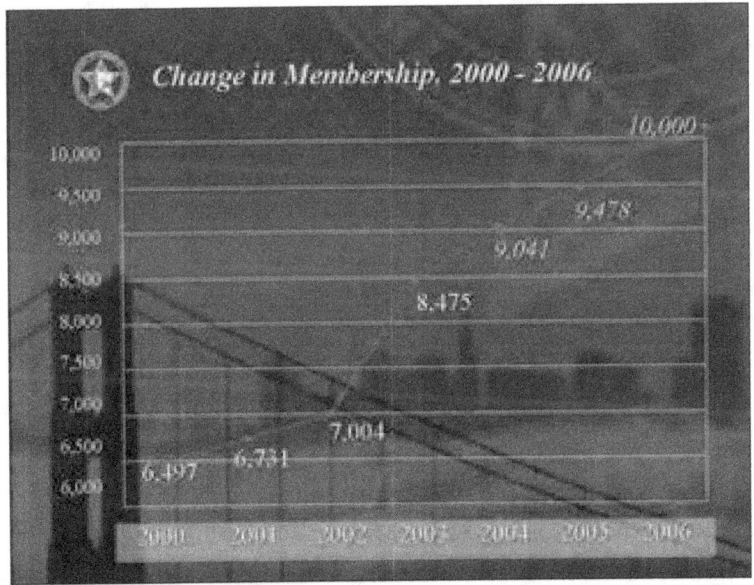

Figure 23. Membership Soars in the Association of American Geographers.
Source: Association of American Geographers.

---

73 Michael F. Goodchild, "Geography Prospers from GIS," *Environmental Systems Research Institute, Inc.*, April 2007, URL: <http://www.esri.com/news/arcwatch/0407/feature.html>, accessed 1 August 2007. Cited hereafter as Goodchild, "Geography Prospers."

that property data, too, can be collected, organized, analyzed, and visualized to support foreign policy decisions. Goodchild continues:

> Several recent advances in geospatial technology have truly caught the popular imagination, starting with wayfinding sites such as MapQuest and progressing to today's Google Earth, Microsoft Virtual Earth, and many more. People are now able to see their own houses and neighborhoods in a global context...People are better equipped to see the relevance of GIS in many aspects of human activity and to appreciate the power that GIS provides to government, the oil and gas industry, disaster management, law enforcement, the military, conservation, and a host of other sectors.[74]

Indeed, from a low point in the 1980s, GIS has not only revived the popularity of geography as an academic discipline, but has become an indispensable tool for other fields. According to Goodchild, GIS is taught in surveying, civil engineering, computer science, anthropology, environmental science, and many other disciplines, particularly on campuses with no department of geography. Most GIS courses are offered through departments of geography, and geographers make up a healthy percentage of the global community of GIS researchers.[75] The resurgence of geography as a discipline is reflected in the 10,000 members in the Association of American Geographers (AAG), a figure which has nearly doubled since 2000.

Bowman Expeditions

The uniqueness of geography is epitomized in a new proposal by Dobson to dispatch place-based geographic research expeditions around the world, a project that has captured the attention and funding of the U.S. Army. Named in honor of former AGS Director Isaiah Bowman, the first Bowman Expedition, called the Mexico Indigena Project and led by Peter Herlihy, Associate Professor of Geography at the University of Kansas (KU), in 2005-06 traced the transfer of property from *ejidos* (a uniquely Mexican form of large landholdings owned communally but cultivated by individual farmers) to private property (see Appendix A. Mexico Indigena Project Cycle). Dobson opines that this project merely foreshadows what geographers can do to convey knowledge of foreign lands, establish relationships with indigenous peoples and institutions, collect unclassified information, and build an open-source GIS that can be employed by other investigators, regardless of discipline. It is but one remedy

46 |

---

74 Goodchild, "Geography Prospers."
75 Goodchild, "Geography Prospers."

to restore geography in its rightful place in higher education and public policy circles. Dobson recalls the genesis of the expedition.

> I wrote a proposal suggesting that most of the missing knowledge about foreign lands is not secret, insider information that should be classified. The AGS can send a geography professor and two or three graduate students to every country in the world for a full semester each year, with teams rotating on a five-year cycle so that each country is understood by five separate teams. I calculated a budget and was shocked myself to realize that the entire program would cost only $125,000,000 per year, a pittance compared to what the IC typically pays for far less effective information. I circulated the proposal and found allies at Ft. Leavenworth, Kansas. They marketed the concept and funded a prototype for the larger concept that, ideally, would reach every country in the world. [76]

An important part of a Bowman Expedition's design is to allow each investigator to choose a research topic for in-depth analysis. Professor Herlihy's research team chose land tenure and uncovered a revolutionary land reform comparable in magnitude to the land reform under the Mexican constitution of 1917 that first created *ejidos*.

> The Program for Certification of *Ejidal* Rights and Titling of [parcels] (PROCEDE) began in 1993 as a Mexican government program to privatize the *ejido* lands. Lands that have been held communally for almost a century are being converted to private property on a massive scale. In a two stage process, each present occupant can apply for a certificate that does not imply actual ownership. After one transfer, say when the farmer dies and the land passes to an offspring, the new holder can apply for an actual title. Henceforth, the parcel can be sold or used as collateral on a loan. The implications are staggering for about 90 percent of the more than 30,000 agrarian communities in the country where PROCEDE has already finished its work, now covering around 100,000,000 hectares or about half of Mexico's land area and including millions of indigenous farmers.[77]

---

76 Jerome E. Dobson, "American Geographical Society (AGS) Conducts Fieldwork in Mexico," *Ubique—Notes from the American Geographical Society (AGS)* 26, no. 1 (2006). Cited hereafter as Dobson, "Fieldwork in Mexico."

77 Dobson, "Fieldwork in Mexico."

Mexico Indigena Project 2005-2006

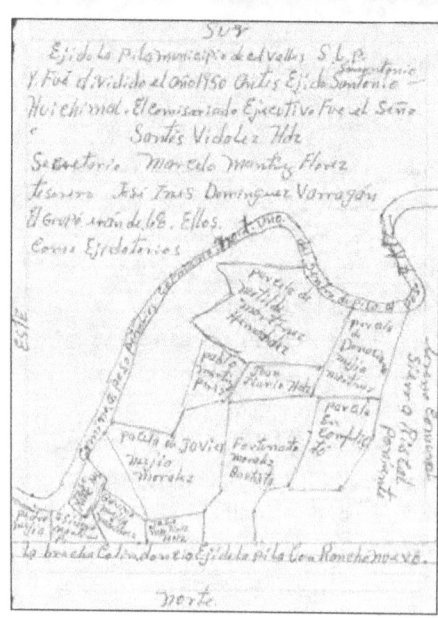

Figure 24. Participants and Figure 25. Sketch Map of Parcels. *Source: Mexico Indigena. http://web. ku.edu/~mexind/index.htm.*

Mexico Indigena Project 2005-2006 (Continued)

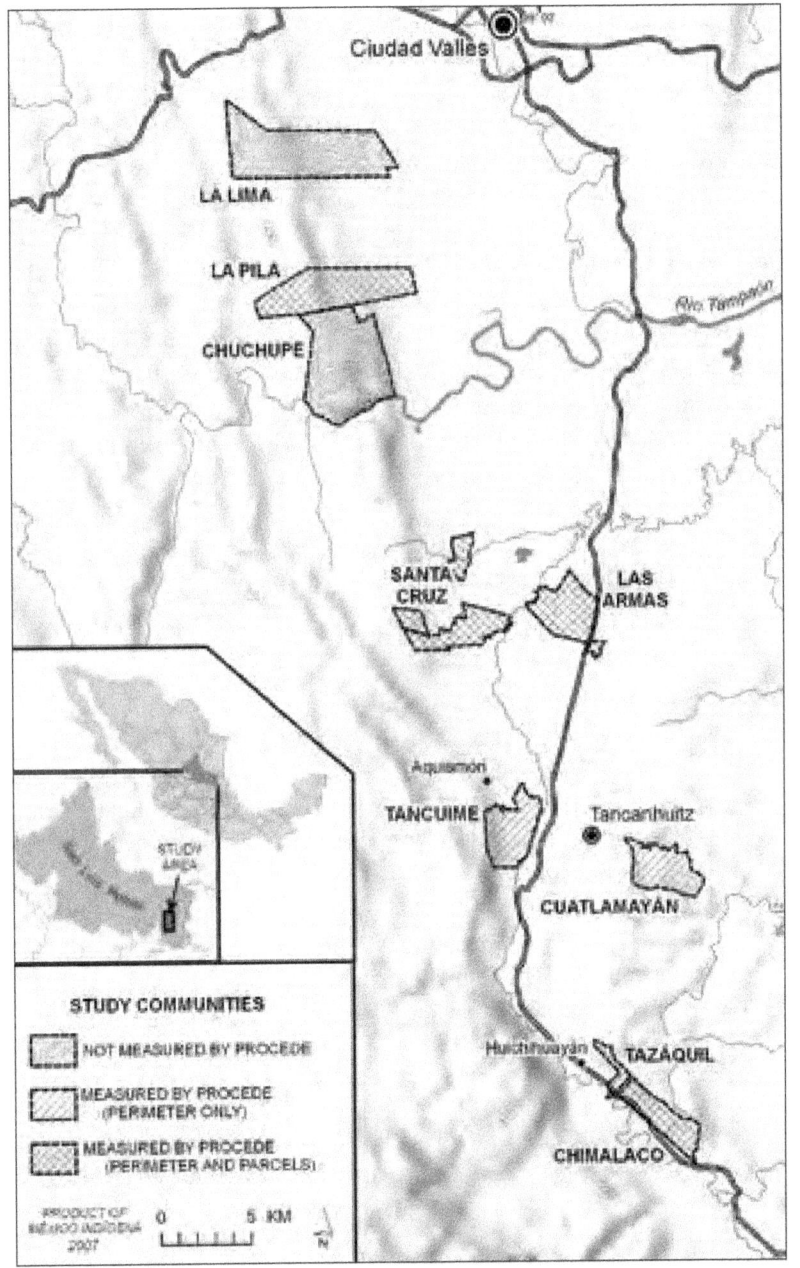

Figure 26. Area Map. *Source: Mexico Indigena.*

An analysis of PROCEDE's effects on the Mexican populace is a perfect example of salient GIS information untapped by the IC. The U.S. Department of Homeland Security's Customs and Border Protection, based on hometowns or origins of detained illegal immigrants where PROCEDE has been enacted, could identify out-migration trends from Mexico and enhance the deployment and effectiveness of border protection resources. While a comparative GIS analysis of the world's various property regimes might be years away, the identification of shortcomings or strengths on which to base property rights revisions is attainable now. In fact, the Mexico Indigena Project had this very purpose in mind. All Bowman Expedition results will be published in open literature, and GIS data will be available on-line because the goal is to inform not just the government, but also the general public via a new type of automated regional geography. Dobson announced that a second Bowman Expedition received Department of Defense funding to conduct fieldwork in the Antilles, an unusual challenge with so many island nations. Over three years, recipients of Bowman Expedition funds to the Antilles will include the following institutions and tasks:[78]

- Kansas State University has accepted primary responsibility for building and maintaining a multi-resolution, open source GIS database for the entire Antilles Region.

- Virginia Tech will conduct a comparative analysis of water resource issues in the Dominican Republic and Haiti.

- Louisiana State University will focus on land-use and land cover dynamics as they relate to tourism, the dominant economic sector in the Leeward segment of the Lesser Antilles.

- Miami and Hofstra Universities will compare and contrast rural economic conditions, land use change, and job prospects in three independent countries of the southern Lesser Antilles.

- Indiana University will conduct field-based research to investigate the consequences of rapid urbanization in Trinidad and rapid coastal zone tourism-related development in Tobago.

- The University of Kansas will coordinate the effort among participants, report to AGS, and interface onsite with the sponsor .

The Bowman Expeditions are only an indication that future endeavors to collect and create cadastral data will not be the domain of central governments alone. Not only are American academicians analyzing property data with GIS,

---

[78] Jerome E. Dobson, "AGS Bowman Expeditions," *The American Geographical Society* (12 June 2007), URL: <http://www.amergeog.org/bowman-expeditions.htm>, accessed 27 June 2007.

but also indigenous peoples, whose rural livelihoods are threatened by insecure tenure and incapacitated governments, are GIS-empowered to locally manage their land matters.

Community/Participatory Mapping

The International Land Coalition (ILC) is a network of intergovernmental, governmental, and civil society organizations that work to increase opportunities for the poor and disadvantaged to participate in decision-making on land tenure security issues. For many rural communities, maps are a step toward grass-roots empowerment for better land access and tenure security. Rural maps, in the experience of ILC's partners, have many times increased the users' capacity to advocate, lobby, plan, manage and monitor the territorial and land-related dimensions of development activities in the mapped areas.[79]

A prime example involved former combatants in the 1980-1992 Salvadoran civil war, in which land tenure was one of the primary causes of a conflict that claimed over 70,000 lives. When post-conflict land transfers from the El Salvadoran government slowed, disaffection rebounded. The government's desire to expedite the land titling process resulted in joint land titles rather than the promised individual ones. "In that situation, everyone owns everything and so no one owns anything."[80] No individual could get credit for loans without the support of the entire group. The original land tenure conflict in El Salvador remained unsolved until the Cooperative for Assistance and Relief Everywhere (CARE) enabled the community to decide how to divide the land into individual plots or into grazing or other communal use lands. With GPS that used laser beams to measure distances, the titling process became transparent and owned by the community. "There was a lot of discussion," said Roberto Candel, CARE's GPS expert, "But once they could see the map, see what decisions they were talking about, they were able to make those decisions."[81]

The Salvadoran case demonstrates that community-produced sketch maps can be combined with GIS to go beyond the determination of primary rights (ownership rights) to include secondary use rights (access to grazing land, water resources, fruit trees and forest) to regularize tenure and to resolve land conflict. In the developing world, "a blend of statutory, customary and hybrid (formal or informal) institutions and regulations may co-exist in the

---

79 Stefano de Gessa, *Participatory Mapping as a Catalyst for Rural People's Empowerment: An Overview of Experiences from the International Land Coalition (ILC) Network* (Rome: International Land Coalition (ILC), April 2006), URL: <www.landcoalition.org/pdf/mapping_ILC.pdf>, accessed 25 September 2007. Cited hereafter as De Gessa, *Participatory Mapping.*

80 De Gessa, *Participatory Mapping.*

81 Douglas Farah, "Satellites Solve Salvadoran Farm Disputes," *The Washington Post,* 14 July 1996.

same territory, all having a *de jure* or *de facto* authority over land rights. Land conflicts, particularly in rural and remote areas, are multi-dimensional and complex."[82]

Geography as a Tangible Foreign Policy Tool

Geography, the discipline that buttressed American eminence in early 20th century world affairs, suffered a decline which contributed to policy makers' inability to fathom that human conflict springs from ruptures in the relationships between land and people. The ethnic origins of post-Cold War conflicts accentuate the significance of geography in foreign policy matters. Geographic education at all levels in the U.S. should be bolstered, similar to the emphasis placed on math and science following the launch of Sputnik. Theories of geography alone, however, are insufficient for decision-making. On the other hand GPS and GIS tools, as employed in field studies such as the Bowman Expeditions and the ILC initiative, can encourage and improve property rights, a most tangible objective for U.S. foreign policy. Both technological developments portend a recovery of geography, namely human geography, as a pillar of intelligence analysis. There is an even more valuable tool to aid in broader foreign policy decisions, one that can capture the multi-dimensional and complex sets of land rights and interests. That tool will be discussed in Chapter 6, but to appreciate its importance, basic principles of land tenure must be understood, the topic of Chapter 5.

---

[82] De Gessa, *Participatory Mapping.*

CHAPTER 5:
Securing the Land: The Pivotal Role of Cadastres in Nation-Building

In medieval Europe a king's realm was his own. It was by the favor of the king that his subordinate nobles and lords held property and territory. Holding—not owning—the land implies a dependence upon the king, not only for his continued permission, but for his protection from those who might try to seize the property. The Latin word *tenere*—to hold—forms the basis of this arrangement, and serves as the root for *tenant, tenement,* and *tenure.* These words, like landlord, are so familiar that their original feudal overtones have been lost.

In the modern West the tenant relationship no longer holds between citizens and the State. Individuals may own their property independent of the government, which normally has property holdings of its own, separate from privately owned property. This is the arrangement in Western countries, but across the world there are various patterns. In developing countries the state may own all land, or it may have a *laissez-faire* policy toward informal property rights—until foreign investors show interest in the land. Common to every country, no matter the political or economic system, no matter whether industrialized or developing, is the notion of land tenure, one of the key concepts of this book.

Land tenure is the relationship, whether legally or customarily defined, among people, as individuals or groups, with respect to land. Land tenure is an institution, i.e., rules invented by societies to regulate behavior. Rules of tenure define how property rights to land are to be allocated within societies. In simple terms, land tenure systems determine who can use what resources for how long, and under what conditions.[83]

As opposed to English Common Law, four European Civil Code principles concerning property rights are: *usus* (to use, but not to financially benefit from), *fructus* (to enjoy the fruit of the land: sell crops, sublet), *abusus* (alienation: the right to sell or transfer ownership), and *accessio* (assets of deceased persons). By rule of law, these principles form the legal basis of cadastres and the registrations of land rights, which must be supported by

---

[83] Food and Agriculture Organization of the United Nations (FAO), *Land Tenure and Rural Development, FAO Land Tenure Studies* (Rome: FAO Publishing Management Service, 2002), 13. Cited hereafter as FAO, *Land Tenure and Rural Development.*

some sort of land representation, the *forma* aspect, i.e., on a cadastral map or a parcel-lot graphic containing a geographic *location*, a parcel *description* (e.g., measures and directions, plain text, metes and bounds, coordinates, township subdivisions), and a *designation* (label, structured or sequentially identifying number).[84] It may be useful to examine property rights by distinguishing three different kinds:[85]

- **Use Rights:** (a combination of *usus* and *fructus* aspects) rights to use and enjoy the land for grazing, growing subsistence crops, gathering minor forestry products, etc.
- **Control Rights:** rights typical of custodianship, the right to make decisions (chiefly *usus*, seldom *abusus*) about how the land should be used, including deciding what crops should be planted, and who should benefit financially (*fructus*) from the sale of crops, etc.
- **Transfer Rights:** typical of ownership, the right to sell or mortgage the land, to convey the land to others through intra-community reallocations, to transmit the land to heirs through inheritance, and to reallocate use and control rights (*accessio* and *abusus*).

There are other rights associated with property, but these three are the chief ones. In a single tract of land these rights may be held by three different parties. Perhaps only in Switzerland is each registered individual property right guaranteed by the State; nevertheless, landowners and other people who enjoy various rights to land still rely upon the state for enforcement of their property rights.

- **Security of Tenure** is the certainty given by a government that a person's various rights to land will be recognized by others and protected from violations.

Security of tenure is taken for granted in the West, but in many parts of the world, particularly in developing countries, millions of people face the risk that their land rights will be threatened by others, and even lost as a result of eviction. The layers of complexity and potential for conflict are compounded when, for example, the state suddenly claims ownership of land long held by people through custom and tradition. Officially, these people are landless. But these "landless" poor care deeply about their property. Even if not legally registered "people invest in turning a tin-sheet house into a concrete house and upgrade their properties. It does not matter that

---

84 Yaïves Ferland, "Geographically Informed Structures (GIS) for Cadastral Representation," paper presented at the 97th annual meeting of the Association of American Geographers (AAG), 1 March 2001 (New York City, NY).

85 FAO, *Land Tenure and Rural Development*.

Figure 27. In Kabul's Informal Settlements Water Vendors Make Deliveries to Homes without Running Water or Wells—or Security of Tenure. *Source: Author.*

they hold the land informally without legally produced individual titles, the wealth of all of these poor people is tied up in their land and housing."[86] Thus, the security with which people hold their lands is crucial for the world's landless poor. Ownership is not as great a concern, because their most immediate worry is forced eviction, whether by the state or a third party. Unfortunately, in the developing world time and expense of issuing and registering titles often undermine the goal of secure tenure for the poor. These "land tenure policies confuse 'ownership' with 'security of tenure,' resulting only in delays in extending effective security of tenure"[87] to those who need it.

Consider, for example, Figure 28, which depicts a typical situation in a developing country. Imagine a well-watered valley. Every spring a family of herders do what their ancestors have done for centuries, bring their

---

86 Allan Cain, *Urban Poverty and Civic Development in Post-War Angola of Preparing for Peace Workshop on Future Swedish and Norwegian Development Cooperation with Angola*, April 2002, URL: <http://www.angonet.org/article.ph?story=20061116174108871&mode=print>, accessed 13 July 2007.

87 Ben Cousins and Rosalie Kingwill, "Land Rights and Cadastral Reform in Post-Apartheid South Africa," paper presented at the 9th International Conference of the Global Spatial Data Infrastructure (GSDI-9), 6-10 November 2006 (Santiago, Chile), URL: <www.gsdi9.cl/english/abstracts/TS26.4abstract.pdf>, accessed 24 July 2007.

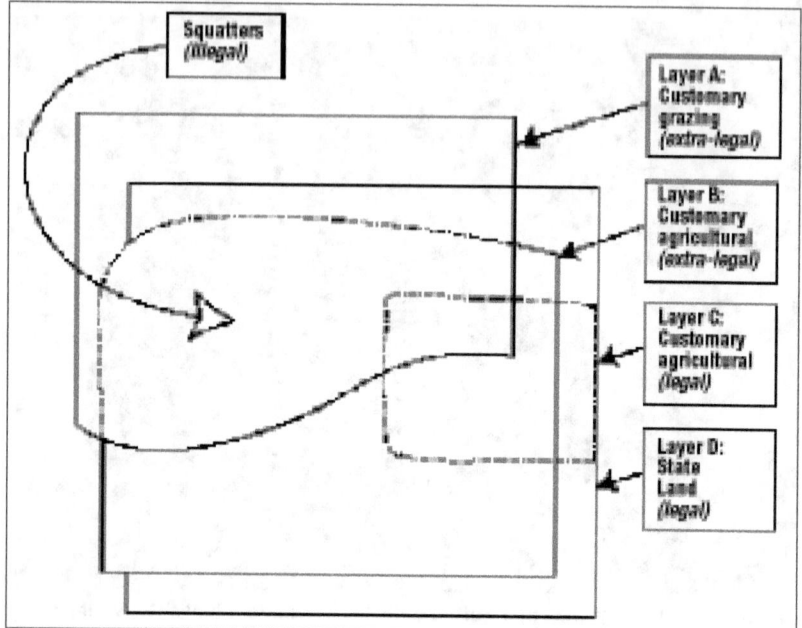

Figure 28: Complexities and Conflicts Resulting from Different Types of Tenure.
Source: Food and Agriculture Organization of the United Nations (FAO), Land Tenure and Rural Development, 3, May 2003.

flocks to pasture in the valley (Layer A in the Figure 28). In that same valley there are farmers practicing their ancestral livelihood (Layer B), who, honoring a longstanding verbal agreement, allow the herders water rights every spring. Recently, a major drought forced a related ethnic group from a neighboring country to settle in the valley. The government does not enjoy friendly relations with the neighboring country and considers these new arrivals illegal squatters. Decades ago, unbeknownst to either the herders or the farmers, the newly emergent government laid claim to the entire valley as state domain (Layer D). The government never attempted to develop the land until now, when a foreign mineral company notified the government of a valuable resource in part of the valley, and negotiated a lease (Layer C). For each of these four parties a different land right is at work.

Responses to tenure insecurity vary according to local contexts, to the size and nature of land invasions and informal settlements; national political leanings; and pressures exerted by civil society, NGOs, and the affected peoples. But overall, there are two main approaches to providing security of tenure, different but not contradictory. The first, typical of

Western societies, conducts tenure regularization based primarily on the conveyance of individual titles, but sometimes also based on public acts and private deeds. The second approach emphasizes an administrative or legal protection against forced eviction. Unlike complicated, expensive, and time-consuming formal tenure regularization programs, under this approach security of tenure can be provided through simple regulatory and normative measures.[88] Fourie lists some use and control rights, which at a later stage, through incremental regularization procedures, can be upgraded to freehold or long-term leases:[89]

- De facto recognition, but without legal status, such as an anti-eviction measure
- Recognition of security of tenure, but without any form of tenure regularization (the authorities certify that the settlement will not be removed)
- Provision of temporary occupancy permits
- Temporary non-transferable leases

Cadastre and Controversy

As mentioned in the Introduction, cadastres are systems of land registration. In a nation where a war or a major catastrophe has displaced large numbers of people, restoring those people to the land is a key part of any serious effort to reconstruct the country. Reconstruction attracts people with a variety of viewpoints. There are various competing theories on cadastres and how to rectify a nation's defective, fragmented, or non-existent land administration system. Regardless of the chosen method or intervention, a cadastre remains for post-conflict planners the primary source of information about the broad spectrum of formal and informal rights and interests in land. Such information includes:[90]

- People who have interests in parcels of land
- Interests in the land, e.g., nature and duration of rights, restrictions and responsibilities

88 Graham Adler, "Ownership Is Not a Priority among the Urban Poor: The Case of Nairobi's Informal Settlements," *Habitat Debate UNCHS--The United Nations Centre for Human Settlements* 5, no. 3 (1999), URL: <http://www.unhabitat.org/hd/hdv5n3/viewpoint.htm>, accessed 24 September 2007.

89 Clarissa Fourie, *"Best Practices Analysis on Access to Land and Security of Tenure"* (Durban, South Africa: University of Natal, 1999), on-line information site of Dr. Clarrisa Augustinus (previous last name Fourie), consultant for UNCHS, also known as UN-HABITAT, URL: <http://www.google.com/search?hl=en&q=Fourie+2B+Best+practices+analysis+on+access+to+land+>, accessed 16 July 2007.

90 FIG, *The FIG Statement on the Cadastre.*

- Basic details about the parcel, e.g., location, size, improvements, value.

Despite their basic utility, cadastres are controversial today. "When a land registrar writes down the name of an owner in a land book, or a land surveyor draws a boundary line on a cadastral map, it could be either the start of a prosperous economic development, or the overture to a new conflict."[91] Some critics say that a classical cadastre, a top-down, state-led approach is best for economic growth because participatory, community-level exercises are not recognized by higher-level planning authorities who see the bigger picture. Others with a grassroots agenda insist upon a citizen cadastre, one that is participatory, affordable, and tenure-securing, that harmonizes informal and customary needs and norms with formal and statutory needs and rules, without which a national land policy can never be credible. The grave concerns and objections raised by some members of the international development community suggest that cadastral surveys have a history of causing, rather than mitigating, conflict and instability.

Cadastres and land tenure reforms associated with them can be threatening, especially to parties who want to maintain a status quo that cements their prestige, power, and profit. Alain Durand-Lasserve and Lauren Royston have no illusions that national decrees or new land policies alone provide security of tenure to the most marginalized of society: the poor, the poorly educated, indigenous peoples, ethnic minorities, and women.

> Slum organizers, political bosses and tribal chiefs can often view tenure regularization as eroding their privileged social and economic position. Municipal officials and ministries that exhibited near absolute power over land decisions do not easily give up control. Political sympathy for squatters is frequently low. Change, which improves the situation for some, will necessarily erode political, cultural, and/or economic power for others. For all these reasons and more, the process is often complicated, political and violent.[92]

True, cadastres can be used to nefarious ends. Conflict is inevitable
58 | when outsiders, a category that includes regional or national governments, conduct or sponsor cadastral surveys supported by foreign investment or

---

91 Paul van der Molen and Christiaan Lemmen, "Land Administration in Post-Conflict Areas," paper presented at the 3rd FIG Regional Conference, 2004 (Jakarta, Indonesia), URL: <www.itc.nl/library/Papers_2004/n_p_conf/vandermolen_land.pdf>, accessed 25 September 2007.

92 Alain Durand-Lasserve and Lauren Royston, *Holding Their Ground: Secure Land Tenure for the Urban Poor in Developing Countries*, ISBN 1853838918 (London: Earthscan Publications Ltd., 2002), 241.

other outside interests that divest local land stakeholders in favor of other parties. Additionally, in many parts of the world, the very word cadastre smacks of ties to colonialism, increased taxation (perceived to benefit only corrupt officials at the expense of sewer, water, electrical, transportation, health, or other services), or to government attempts to expropriate land from indigenous peoples. Thus, the neutral term of land administration is supplanting the word *cadastre*, especially in Europe. In reality, a cadastre is theoretically neutral. The problem in post-conflict societies is that cadastres have been designed to serve the interests of governments and outside powers, not the local people, who are usually poor. If a cadastre does not reflect local arrangements concerning the land, it is open to abuse, particularly in post-conflict countries. Cadastres in these situations should be designed to be flexible, registering all land claims, including competing ones. From a comprehensive repository of land information, tenure decisions can be made efficiently and equitably. The cadastre then becomes multi-purpose. As the rebuilding nation develops the capacity to resettle refugees, adjudicate land claims, and provide economic and other incentives to maintain the cadastre, a key foundation of civil society takes root.

In stable Western countries the cadastre reflects the land policies of the central government, and it falls at the bottom of a well-ordered hierarchy. At the top is the land management system, which develops a national land policy and strategy. The land administration system, next in the hierarchy, implements the policy and strategy. Beneath that fall various subsystems: land tenure, taxation, utilities, and so forth. Finally comes the cadastre, which records boundary lines, surveyors' reports, land registration, and claims to land.[93] Augustinus and Barry identify this as the conventional approach to land management, an arrangement adequate for most stable countries. But, they argue, post-conflict societies cannot follow this positivist model without incurring massive delay and expense and prolonging and exacerbating the land crises they are meant to address. They advocate a soft-systems approach, where the traditional top-down hierarchy becomes adjustable according to ever-changing local needs. If tenure issues are pressing, the land tenure system can be prioritized over land management and land administration. If the local situation changes yet again, any other system can come to the fore.

For soft systems, a cadastre remains central, just as it is in the conventional approach, but it should not be centralized. The tendency in many

| 59

---

93 Clarissa Augustinus and Michael B. Barry, "Land Management Strategy Formulation in Post-Conflict Societies," *Survey Review* 38, no. 302, ISSN 0039-6265 (October 2006), 10. Cited hereafter as Augustinus and Barry, "Land Management Strategy."

international aid or development enterprises is to design a cadastre to fit the needs of a local settlement, then to take that model to a national level and attempt to create a single overarching cadastral system that can suit every part of the country and take into account existing land policy. In post-conflict societies "land policy is being developed at the local settlement [level]"[94] and cadastres must record what is happening there and then, not wait for a national land policy to take shape.

The Rural Lands Administration Project (RLAP) in Afghanistan advocates a similar approach, patiently seeking in post-conflict society the "empowerment of people at the local level to manage their land relations themselves."[95] Just as Augustinus and Barry advocate a soft systems approach over a positivist one in post-conflict societies, J. David Stanfield of RLAP argues that the application of formal law to adjudicate claims to land through government officials consigns communities to a diminished role, and even then only in the final validation of findings by outsiders. In the Afghan context, "where a local consensus exists about the rights people have to land, that local definition is the starting point to define rights and rules."[96] Furthermore, reasons Stanfield:

> A community administration of property records is the place to start searching for answers. By "community administration" we mean the actual administration by community people of property records, and not a District Office of a central land registry receiving petitions for land information or for recording transactions, nor a District Office sending a team once in a while to communities to gather evidence of transactions. As in the case of land, people feel more secure in their documentation of their rights to land when they "own" their land records, that is, when they control access to these records. When this security exists people invest in the maintenance and usefulness of land records.[97]

---

94 Augustinus and Barry, "Land Management Strategy."

95 Liz Alden Wily, *Governance and Land Relations: A Review of Decentralisation of Land Administration and Management in Africa*, ISBN 1-84369-496-4 (London: International Institute for Environment and Development (IIED), 2003), 1. Cited hereafter as Alden-Wiley, *Governance and Land Relations.*

96 J. David Stanfield, "Community Recording of Property Rights: Focus on Afghanistan," paper presented to the International Association of Clerks, Recorders, Election Officials and Treasurers (IACREOT) 2007 Annual Conference and Trade Show, 19 July 2007 (Charlotte, North Carolina). Cited hereafter as Stanfield, "Community Recording."

97 Stanfield, "Community Recording."

As noted anthropologist Liz Alden-Wiley states, "only when land administration and management is fully devolved to the community level... is there likely to be significant success in bringing the majority of land interests under useful and lasting record-centered management."[98]

Cadastres Help Rebuild Shattered Nations

One of the world's poorest countries suffered a devastating civil war that ended in 2002 after nearly three decades. The war killed up to one and a half million people and displaced four million more, destroyed much of the country's infrastructure, and left a deadly legacy of landmines, which have maimed an estimated 80,000 people. When the conflict ended, perhaps three percent of the arable land was under cultivation, two million people were on the brink of starvation, and three million received direct humanitarian assistance.[99]

The country in question is surprisingly not Afghanistan, but Angola. In both countries, as humanitarian relief gives way to broad-based development, a national land policy is sorely needed. The laws currently on the books in Angola, based upon the outdated Portuguese colonial cadastre, are inadequate to provide security of tenure. "Many of Land Law 1992 (Law 21-C/92) provisions were not enforced and it soon became clear to most observers that the legal framework it provided was inadequate."[100]

One agent for reform is Development Workshop (DW), an NGO present in Angola since 1981 with "programs for shelter, peri-urban upgrading, water supply and sanitation, microfinance and small enterprise development, peace-building, governance, and disaster mitigation."[101] The efforts of DW, the Food and Agriculture Organization of the United Nations (FAO), and a network of NGOs known as the *Rede Terra* helped pass needed amendments to the flawed 1992 law. The 2004 Angolan Land Act Number 09/04, with rights recorded in a new cadastre, provides some protection from arbitrary evictions and government land expropriations prompted by

---

98 Alden-Wiley, *Governance and Land Relations*.

99 Conor Foley, Land Rights in Angola, (London, England: Overseas Development Institute, 2007). Cited hereafter as Foley, Land Rights in Angola.

100 Foley, Land Rights in Angola.

101 Developmental Workshop, Contributing to Poverty Reduction in Angola, 31 December 2005, URL: <http://www.dw.angonet.org/>, under the keywords "poverty" and "Angola", accessed 19 July 2007.

increasing Chinese investments.[102] As a hedge against encroaching commercial interests that threaten traditional livelihoods, the Norwegian Refugee Council (NRC) in Angola educates a mostly illiterate population about their land rights under the new law.

Another post-conflict nation aided in its return to stability by a reformed cadastre is Cambodia. Their cadastre is a model for being at once low cost, digital, and thoroughly integrated. Few countries' needs are as great as Cambodia's.

> Cambodians have suffered through a tumultuous recent history, during which the rules for rights to land have been in constant flux.... The Khmer Rouge, which came to power in 1975, collectivized all land and destroyed all land records, including cadastral maps and titles. The right to own land was re-established in 1989.... In 1992, a program was initiated calling for applications for land tenure certificates to confirm occupancy and use rights. More than four million applications were submitted, but only 15 percent of them had been processed due to limited capacity of government. A lack of national policies related to land, inadequate organizational structure, lack of educated professionals and equipment hindered and delayed establishment of land register.[103]

The trauma Cambodia suffered included the gutting of its technically trained workforce. Concerted international efforts ultimately led in 2002 to a Land Management and Administration Project (LMAP) that took local capacity and resources into account. Rather than professionally train a cadastral staff for four or more years, LMAP mobilized 300 Cambodians and taught them for 18-36 months to become cadastral technicians. In a relatively short time LMAP implemented the first Cambodian land registration and multipurpose digital cadastre. It aspires to cover the entire country and issue seven million land titles in 10 to 15 years.

Higher accuracy cadastral surveys for urban areas are conducted with total station traverse, lower accuracy surveys with orthophotograph inter-

102 Conrad Hendry, "China's Challenging Investment in Angola," Hong Kong Trade and Development Council (28 March 2006), URL: <http://www.tdctrade.com/imn/06032804/investment037.htm.>, accessed 19 July 2007.

103 Pertti Onkalo, "Cadastral Survey Methodologies and Techniques in Developing Countries; Case Cambodia and Kosovo," paper TS-61presented at the 23rd International FIG Congress, 8-13 October 2006 (Munich, Germany), URL: <www.fig.net/pub/fig2006/papers/ts61/ts61_02_onkalo_0318.pdf>, accessed 25 September 2007. Cited hereafter as Onkalo, "Cadastral Survey Methodologies."

pretation and digitization. Land owners often serve as field assistants, which improves their understanding of the cadastral surveys and, with the public posting of the cadastral index maps, reduces the number and intensity of boundary disputes. "Accuracy cannot be a top priority, especially not in rural areas where land values are low. Also for the buildings, high accuracy is not essential and sometimes even the location point could be enough."[104]

In most parts of the developing world high registration fees, unaffordable to the poor, perpetuate informal, unregistered property transactions. This, in turn, undermines the accuracy of a new cadastre, which comes at no small cost anywhere in the world. Moreover, if the government plans to fund the land registry from user fees, as is the case in Cambodia, failure to convince landowners to use the cadastre for property registration and subsequent transactions results in an overpriced, incomplete (and therefore useless) database. Cambodia's LMAP has been a success: 15 years of substantial international and donor support has kept the cost for registering a title low. In rural areas of Cambodia the registry cost per parcel is $6.20; in urban areas $17.41, among the cheapest in the world (see Table 1). For an average of $8.74 per parcel, property registration in Cambodia includes title production, materials, and salaries, but not equipment and aerial photography.[105]

Country	Cost Per Parcel in USD in 2006
Cambodia	8.74
Moldova	9.90
Peru (urban)	12.66
Kyrgyzstan	15.76
Albania	18.00
Armenia	18.02
Indonesia	24.40
Thailand	32.80
Peru (rural)	46.86
Trinidad and Tobago	1,064.00
Latvia (sporadic)	1,356.00

Table 1. Average Cost Per Parcel in Systematic Registration in Developing Countries. *Source: Onkalo, 2006.*

104 Onkalo, "Cadastral Survey Methodologies."
105 Onkalo, "Cadastral Survey Methodologies."

Figure 29. 1:5000 Scale-Delineated Satellite Images. The boundaries of forest and pasture parcel boundaries have been delineated. *Source: Terra Institute.*

Finer spatial accuracies needed in urban areas of Cambodia can be obtained at a later date, funded by user fees from the parties involved. Similarly, land disputes that needlessly hinder a cadastre's completion can be registered as completing claims as part of the cadastral survey. A resolution may come all the sooner when the dispute is made part of the public record.

Like Cambodia, Ethiopia changed radically in 1975. In this case the government nationalized all rural land with the intent to distribute land rights more equitably. Unfortunately, continued changes in tenure laws, a growing rural population, and a shortage of land have led to markedly insecure land tenure for many. This has undermined investment in agriculture, destabilized agricultural output, and contributed to land degradation.[106]

Cadastres have become an important element in rectifying Ethiopia's complex problems. Land Administration Specialist Lennart Bäckstrom oversaw a three-year pilot in the Amhara region of Ethiopia in which a Land

64 |

---

[106] United Nations Environmental Programme (UNEP) World Resources, the United Nations Development Programme (UNDP), the World Bank, and the World Resources Institute (WRI), *The World Resources 2005--the Wealth of the Poor,* 11, Ch. 3 (2005), URL: <http://multimedia. wri.org/wr2005/023.htm>. Accessed 31 March 2007.

Administration System (LAS) thwarted land-grabbers by registering 2.4 million cases of rights and interests in state-owned rural lands and issuing 1.3 million occupancy certificates. The extensive project included the training of 1000 District-level civil servants and 200 lawyers on the legal system, surveying and mapping techniques, and property valuation and real property and user registries. A 2005 World Bank mission lauded the Amhara LAS for its transparency, the high degree of community participation and low cost of certification. "The most important part to development was to define tenure security in user rights, but not mix it with ownership."[107]

But not all has gone well in Ethiopia. Its experience shows that, without the right infrastructure in place a cadastre may be only partially effective. In 2004, masters degree students Fella, Jensen, and Knudsen, sought to learn, "Will the formalization of land tenure, assisted by the GIS project, benefit the current informal settlers within Addis Ababa?" The results, both positive and negative, were uneven. While improvements in city planning were evident, numerous obstacles prevented any actual improvement in basic services to settlers. These obstacles included the inefficiency of municipal staffs and the ill-defined roles within the various government bureaus. "The formalization process did lead to an increased sense of security related to land tenure for the informal settlers and it was found that tenure security is very important for investments in housing improvements. This means that tenure security is an essential spur for the magnitude of investment and quality of housing transformation in the informal settlements in Addis Ababa. The increased tenure security leading to investment in housing is certainly a benefit for the informal settlers."[108] Nevertheless, the increase in taxation and the improvement in planning and administration never translated into better services for the informal settlers.

An even better example of a well-designed but poorly used cadastre is Kosovo, where ethnic conflict resulted in the deliberate destruction of property records. Prompt support from Sweden, Norway, and Switzerland facilitated the construction of a state-of-the-art electronic cadastre. In this cadastre a common parcel ID number links the graphical orthophotos and vectorized cadastral plans in the Kosovo Cadastre and Land Information System (KCLIS) with the textual information found in the Immovable

---

107 Lennart Bäckstrom, "Look at Ethiopia! A Simplified and Result Oriented Development and Implementation of a Low Cost Land Administration System," paper TS-61 presented at the 23rd International FIG Congress, 8-13 October 2006 (Munich, Germany), URL: <www.fig.net/pub/fig2006/papers/ts61/ts61_01_backstrom_0312.pdf>, accessed 24 September 2007.

108 Tim Fella, Kim Jensen, and Martin Knudsen, "Consequences of the Formalization of Informal Settlements in Addis Ababa," (Aalborg, Denmark: Aalborg University, 2004). Cited hereafter as Fella, Jensen and Knudsen, "Consequences."

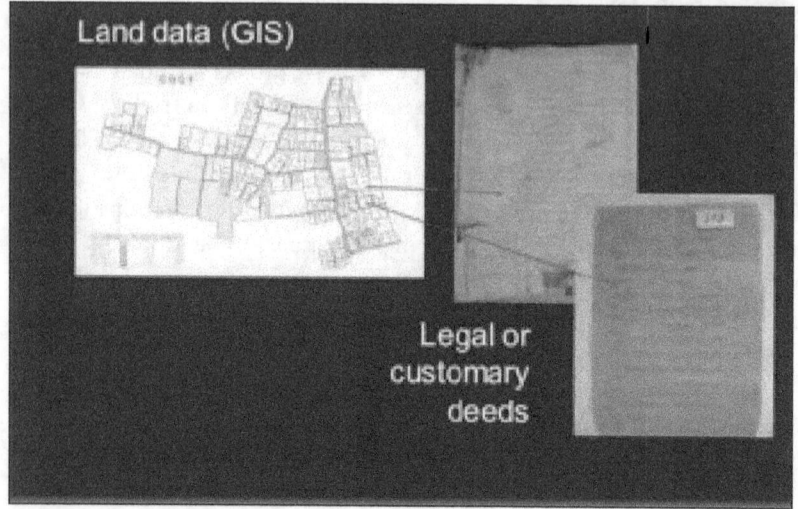

Figure 30. Customary Deeds. *Source: LTERA.*

Property Rights Register (figure 30).[109] All the data are integrated and made available to users through the Internet. The Kosovar e-cadastre enables the visualization of areas where documentation of land ownership or rights is missing or has been destroyed.[110] But because the cadastral system was modernized apart from a supporting land policy, Kosovo's land information systems are unsustainable.[111]

Cadastres Aiding Post-Conflict Afghanistan

Little assistance in settling land disputes and registering rights and interests in lands is forthcoming from the Afghan national government, and even less from the meagerly resourced provincial and district governments. Thus, moving beyond the morass requires initiative at the community level. Nearly all Afghan pastureland, while state-owned, is customarily managed by families, clans, or tribes, and not by private owners. These parties, settled agricultural families and also nomads, raise livestock and gather fuel and medicinal herbs on semi-arid pastures. The locally devised agreements about who has rights to these lands for what purposes during what time of the year have never been recorded.

---

109 Fella, Jensen and Knudsen, " "

110 Murat Meha, "Effects of E-Cadastre in Land Administration in Kosovo and in Other Post Conflict Countries," paper TS-50 presented at the 23rd International FIG Congress, 8-13 October 2006 (Munich, Germany), URL: <www.fig.net/pub/fig2006/papers/ts50/ts50_01_murat_0392.pdf>, accessed 25 September 2007.
Augustinus and Barry, "Land Management Strategy."

111 Augustinus and Barry, "Land Management Strategy."

Most rural families, and also many urban ones, do not use the formal, court-prepared title deeds to document property transactions. Yet the lack of court-prepared documents does not leave Afghans who conduct business informally without any form of tenure security. Customary arrangements, even verbal agreements, witnessed by family members and respected elders have sufficed for centuries because most dealings are inheritance matters and intra-family or intra-tribal agreements. Non-related persons privately draft documents, again witnessed by locally respected people, which are retained by the parties to the transaction without the involvement of any government official.[112]

In response to increasing insecurity of tenure on Afghan rangelands, which occurred only in recent post-conflict years, an RLAP team—funded by the Asian Development Bank and the U.K. Department for International Development (ADB/DfID) and administered through the auspices of Afghanistan's Ministry of Agriculture, Irrigation and Livestock—has created a community-based initiative to produce and record community agreements about who has the legitimate rights to use pasture lands for particular purposes during specific times of the year. Local land stakeholders agree in writing on the legitimate uses and users of pasturelands, delineate boundaries using satellite imagery, and develop plans for improving productivity of defined parcels of rangeland. Following the customary signing and witnessing by village elders, often including local leaders known as *maliks* or *arbabs*, the documents are archived in the village with copies sent to government land institutions. There is trust in this system for several reasons: 1) because local leaders have indicated their concurrence with the agreements, 2) the documents describing legitimate use rights are kept in village archives; 3) the agreements are facilitated by the efforts of educated *maliks* to represent the local people in court disputes or in dealings with government agencies and other outside organizations.

The RLAP initiative has summarized the tested procedures for producing the rangeland agreements with the acronym A-D-A-M-A P:[113]

*A*sk for community cooperation.

*D*elineate the boundaries of rangeland parcels.

*A*greements are prepared concerning the legitimate users of the rangeland parcels.

*M*eet, discuss and approve the agreements and delineations.

*A*rchive the agreements and delineated images.

*P*lan for the improvement of the rangeland parcels.

---

112 Stanfield, "Community Recording."
113 Stanfield, "Community Recording."

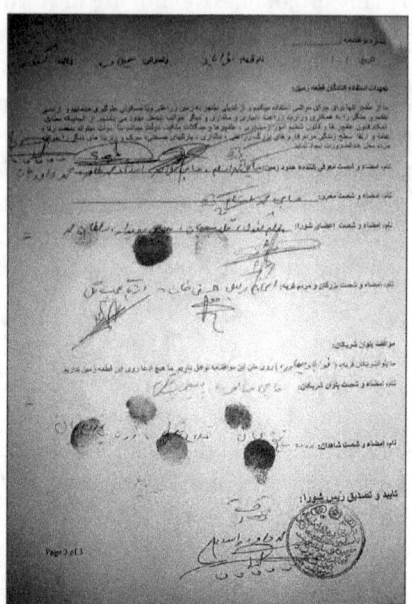

Figure 31. A Signed Pasture Land Agreement. *Source: Terra Institute.*

There have been discussions of expanding RLAP's rangeland agreements into a national effort. RLAP's method has resulted in increased security of tenure and a decrease in rangeland disputes. Village leaders may desire a similar approach to council-supervised identification of private agricultural lands. Satellite imagery identifies parcel boundaries; forms noting ownership and other rights to the parcels are prepared, signed, witnessed, and retained by the village councils (*shuras* or *jirgas*) with copies sent to provincial government agencies.

Nomadic peoples have serious problems with access to land for feeding and watering their flocks. Traditional seasonal migration routes are often being interrupted in Afghanistan by local militia commanders trying to stop nomads from traveling their traditional routes to and from mountain pastures in the summer. To counteract these demands with evidence of long-term traditional easements, steps are being taken by the nomads to document those routes. GPS information facilitates the negotiations of agreements with villagers for rights of passage.[114]

Addressing the pasturelands experience and the incremental step to extend the method to agricultural lands with ADAMAP, Stanfield concludes:

> The legitimization of rights to pasture lands, a potentially very complicated process, shows that community definition of such rights is entirely feasible and normally quickly accomplished. Moreover, villagers are quite willing to keep those records and commit to updating the agreements when the conditions change requiring changes in the written agreements. Taking that experience another step and

---

114 Stanfield, "Community Recording."

Figure 32. Villagers Review a Delineated Satellite Image of Pasture Land Parcels. *Source: Terra Institute.*

applying the same principles of community legitimization of property rights to agricultural land showed that the generation of property records at the community level is not only feasible but that village elders are organizing to do the work themselves, using the satellite imagery provided to them.[115]

Advances in Land Administration in Afghanistan

Community-based creation and maintenance of land rights records is a bottom-up response to weak state institutions. Centralized land-governing institutions in particular have not enjoyed public confidence. With participative, transparent, and observable processes of community recording of locally derived agreements about the legitimate users of rangeland, the RLAP team substantially supports the words of Alden Wily: "Democratization of land administration and management should be an objective of all countries... the more accessible, useable and used, cheaper, speedier and generally more efficient the system will be."[116]

Community-based mapping in rural Afghanistan needs all the help it can get. To this end a valuable resource, eclipsed by a quarter century of conflict, exists intact. While conducting research in Kabul, the author

| 69

---

115 Stanfield, "Community Recording."

116 Alden-Wiley, *Governance and Land Relations.*

Figure 33. Kuchi Herders in Afghanistan Learn about GPS. *Source: Terra Institute.*

visited the Afghan Geodesy and Cartography Head Office (AGCHO) and met Engineer (Eng.) M. Yasin Safar, a retired chief of the AGCHO cadastral department. Safar informed the author that between 1965 and 1978, one-third of Afghan agricultural lands, 12.9 million *jerib* (a traditional unit of land that equals 1/5 hectare, 2000 square meters, or 0.494 acre), were professionally surveyed by the Cadastral Survey. This enormous undertaking, covering 25,800 square kilometers, nearly the size of Rwanda, was not used in a land registration system or in issuance of formal titles. Cadastral surveyors compiled names of probable parcel owners to dispel any notion that they were also official government title adjudicators. Despite their age today, these painstakingly assembled graphical and textual records survived the wars and could contribute to a future land administration system. Owners and occupants certainly have changed but not so for most of the parcel boundaries. There have been few subdivisions and consolidations, at least in the study village.[117] See Appendix B for samples of the AGCHO cadastral survey forms.

Eng. Safar suggests a three-level strategy for establishing a modern land administration system in Afghanistan. His plan, summarized here, appears in its entirety in Appendix C:[118]

---

117 M. Yasin Safar, retired chief of the Cadastral Survey Department of the Afghan Geodesy and Cartography Head Office (AFCHO), interview by the author, 10 March 2007. Cited hereafter as Safar personal interview.

118 Safar personal interview.

Figure 34. A Garbage-strewn Dirt Road in Kabul's District 7. *Source: Author.*

1. Improve the technical capacity for mapping property.

2. Decentralize the Property Records Administration.

3. Build a national technical and financial property information infrastructure to support this local property information administrative infrastructure.

Eng. Safar recounts favorable experience in recording and archiving property transaction documents at the village level, with elders supervising and verifying record updates and maintenance. He suggests that if done properly, the documents so recorded will be given a preferential legal status by local judges in claims presented to them, over claims without such documents.[119]

Nearly 3 million Kabulites live in informal urban settlements lacking security of tenure and the most basic of services: sewer systems, potable water, electricity, roads, schools, and health clinics. The squalor in Kabul's informal settlements is very real. Nevertheless Kabul's informal residents

---

119 Safar personal interview.

Figure 35. With no open spaces in the densely-populated informal settlements, children play in a dilapidated graveyard in Kabul's District 7. *Source: Author.*

have invested an estimated $1 billion in their neighborhoods[120] — an indication that informal settlers care creditably about their homes.

In Afghanistan's growing urban areas, informal property transactions and informal settlements/squatter towns are legion. The legal route is too riddled with bureaucratic obstacles to be viable. In a Terra Institute report J. David Stanfield, Jonathan Reed, and Eng. M. Yasin Safar outlined the 25 cumbersome steps required to legally register a deed for a house purchased in Kabul.[121] More importantly, they recommend improvements to the current practice which deters many from formally registering property transactions.

In the same spirit, at the January 2006 Afghan Conference on Informal Settlements and Tenure Issues, Dr. Djalalzada, the Deputy Minister of Urban Development stated, "the formation of informal settlements demon-

---

[120] Afghan Ministry of Urban Development (MOUD), "White Paper on Tenure Security and Community Based Upgrading in Kabul," paper presented at the Conference on Informal Settlements and Tenure Issues, 15 March 2006 (Kabul, Afghanistan).

[121] J. David Stanfield, Jonathan Reed, and M. Yasin Safar, *Description of Procedures for Producing Legal Deeds to Record Property Transactions in Afghanistan* in *Asia and Near East Reports*, prepared under contract with USAID (Mount Horeb, WI: Terra Institute, Ltd., 2005), URL: <http://www.terrainstitute.org/reports.html>, accessed 24 September 2007. Cited hereafter as Stanfield, Reed and Safar, Producing Legal Deeds.

Figure 36. A scribe assists illiterate and semi-literate countrymen through one of the twenty-five steps required to legally register a property. *Source: Terra Institute.*

strates a weakness of [the formal system] which has been unable to provide land plots to poor people despite the availability of thousands of hectares of vacant lands. It could be argued that the formation of informal settlements has been as much a solution [to housing returnees] as it is a problem."[122]

Land Policy in Afghanistan

Dr. Yohannes Gebremedhin, formerly USAID/Land Titling and Economic Restructuring of Afghanistan (LTERA), Land Titling/Legal Team Leader, and now advisor to the Afghan Ministry of Agriculture, has advised a Land Working group in preparing a draft national land policy to be approved by the entire Afghan cabinet, which would enable the following urban land conditions to be addressed with an overarching strategy[123] (at this writing the policy has been approved by three line ministries and by the Economic Commission of the Cabinet):

---

122 Stanfield, Reed and Safar, Producing Legal Deeds.

123 Yohannes Gebremedhin, *Legal Issues Pertaining to Land Titling and Registration in Afghanistan*, prepared by Land Titling and Economic Restructuring in Afghanistan (LTERA) Project for USAID Review (Kabul, Afghanistan, 2006), 12, URL: <http://www.terrainstitute.org/reports. html>, accessed 25 September 2007. Cited hereafter as Gebremedhim, *Legal Issues*.

Figure 37. Parties to an Afghan Land Dispute. *Source: Department of Defense.*

1. Residents living in informal settlements do not hold registered title. Property in informal settlements may have been acquired by squatter settlements built on public lands; settlements built on privately owned land; settlements built on grabbed land or land bought from land grabbers. In order for residents in informal settlements to obtain formal deeds the legal issues surrounding the mode of land acquisition must be clarified.

2. Many properties are occupied on the basis of customary (informal) deeds; others are based upon multiple claims. The existing registration process is also an adjudication process. Afghanistan needs a separate coherent land registration law. It also needs a land adjudication law that establishes a process by which claims of interests over land are evaluated, conflicting claims resolved and customary settlements recognized.

3. In addition, and critical to the registration process, is the necessity to clarify the legal authority for land mapping, surveying, and related activities in Afghanistan. Improvement of land tenure security is an essential element to peace building in Afghanistan.

4. Land grabbing, particularly in urban areas, has given rise to an extensive informal real estate market. Individuals have appropriated, sub-divided, and distributed public land using the informal market. The ease with which informal land transactions take place discourages formalization of property titles and makes provision of services in urban areas very difficult and complicated for the municipality.

5. The excessive judicial and administrative steps and archaic modes of operation which exist in the system of transfer of real property rights are cumbersome, inefficient and often riddled with corruption. The real property transfer tax, coupled with the unavoidable illegal fees (bribes) at every step in the process, is sufficiently onerous as to discourage legally recognized title registration. More often than not, individuals resort to only using the informal system.

The adoption of a national land policy would establish the foundation for a desperately needed National Land Administration Agency,

Figure 38. An NRC Counselor Explains the Information Counseling and Legal Aid (ICLA) Program to Afghan Villagers. *Source: Author.*

distinct from the entity now administering rural land records and state-owned lands. Resting on the national land policy, a consolidated Land Administrative System could formalize land tenure, integrate formal and informal processes to register property freely, and link cadastral with other maps to create a parcel-based cadastre. Such lofty goals in a stable and well-resourced environment would take years to achieve, in Afghanistan two decades at a minimum, even assuming that the insurgency completely disappears. Like any mammoth undertaking, the way forward is by incremental steps.

Legal Aid in Afghanistan

One step that cannot be overlooked in achieving tenure security is dispute resolution. As a guest of the Norwegian Refugee Council (NRC), the author witnessed NRC's Information Counseling and Legal Aid (ICLA) program counselors resolve land disputes. In addition to shelter, aid distribution, education, and (refugee and IDP) camp management, the NRC employs Afghan nationals as legal specialists and counselors. Free of charge, the ICLA has helped tens of thousands of people regain their land.[124] The ICLA wisely does not import Western notions of jurisprudence, and the staff is highly skilled in handling small cases. Parties to

---

124 Foley, *Housing, Land and Property Restitution Rights.*

a dispute, once satisfied that their case—often perceived to be against a socially more powerful opponent—has been heard, are then encouraged to accept arbitration from a traditional *jirga* or *shura*.

Foley, a former program manager of the ICLA, believes that *jirgas*, in which all neighborhood or village males participate, or the more restrictive *shuras*, comprising select elders, "are the closest thing to democratic institutions in Afghanistan today. They can reach decisions much faster than the official courts, are virtually cost-free, are less susceptible to bribery and are accessible to illiterate Afghans."[125] The ICLA earns legitimacy by infusing traditional, community-based dispute resolution institutions with vitality and with the added prestige of an "international" endorsement. Militia commanders and other power brokers may behave more civilly, and there may be less bloodshed, due to the international status of the NRC representatives. Yet Foley has no misconceptions about the paucity of justice in Afghanistan.

> Such initiatives may help individuals, and may even have a role to play in strengthening civil society and holding the authorities to account, but they are no substitute for an effective justice system based on respect for the rule of law and human rights. Many of NRC's clients have still not obtained justice, and managing people's expectations is becoming an increasing problem. The organization's successes may attract more cases than the centers can handle.[126]

125 Conor Foley, "Legal Aid for Returnees: The NRC Programme in Afghanistan," *Humanitarian Exchange*, March 2004, URL: <http://www.odihpn.org/report.asp?id=2610>, accessed 24 September 2007. Cited hereafter as Foley, "Legal Aid for Returnees."

126 Foley, "Legal Aid for Returnees."

A USAID Project Makes Progress

The Land Titling and Economic Restructuring of Afghanistan (LTERA) Project, USAID-funded and implemented by Emerging Markets Group (EMG), has presented a five-pronged integrated approach to land titling and economic restructuring efforts:[127]

- Land Registration System
- Mapping and Land Information System
- Tenure Regularization
- Policy and Legal Framework
- Release of Public Land

The project has done important work in rehabilitating and reorganizing deeds in Provincial Court archives although little progress has been made in simplifying land titling procedures, clarifying the property rights legal framework, reducing the cost of transactions, or reorganizing land administration agencies. A complete listing of LTERA projects in Afghanistan is at www.ltera.org. Two of their projects are worth special consideration: the upgrading of informal settlements in two districts of Kabul, and the *Makhzan* rehabilitation program.

Figure 39. LTERA's Pilot Project in Kabul District 7. *Source: LTERA.*

---

127 Gebremedhin, *Legal Issues*.

LTERA's Effort to Upgrade Informal Settlements in Kabul Districts 7 and 13

LTERA selected two Community Development Councils (CDCs) that were established by UN-HABITAT in two *gozars* (neighborhoods) in Districts 7 and 13. This decision occurred in part because the community had already established representative bodies (*shuras*) and both residents and the municipality were willing to participate in the program. Although the *shuras* had been involved in previous upgrading projects, the issue of tenure security had not been addressed prior to the LTERA project's program. In District 13, newly established land clarification boards review property deeds presented by the informal settlers. Ninety-five percent of these are informal, customary deeds. Disputes settled at the community level avoid the bureaucratic and uncertain procedures of the Kabul courts. Once community consensus is reached about who lives where or who has the right to live where, LTERA requests a municipality to issue a "certificate of comfort." While not a property deed, it is a valuable form of tenure security.[128]

Out of this pilot effort to formalize informal settlements, LTERA has developed preliminary proposals to create a legal basis for regularizing tenure in other such contexts. The team has developed a replicable and cost-effective methodology that upgrades basic services, regularizes tenure, and formally integrates informal settlements into the municipality's urban planning process. The projects in Districts 7 and 13 are testing an incremental, community-based method of upgrading and tenure regularization. These neighborhoods were chosen because their problems were obvious. Informal settlers lived in fear of forced eviction and therefore had no incentive to improve their dwellings, start businesses, or upgrade their neighborhoods. An LTERA employee informed the author:

> We estimate that in Districts 7 and 13, the implementation of the 1978 Kabul Master Plan would result in evicting 2000 households (about 14,000 people). We are preparing a land use plan for the Districts. The plan contains alternative land development options which better reflect current land patterns, provide residents access to basic services, and consider

---

128 "Providing Land Tenure Security in Afghanistan," *LTERA*, 2007, URL: <http://www.ltera.org/USAID_LTERA_LAND_TENURE.html#Teaming_Up_With_the_World_Bank_KURP_Program_>, accessed 7 August 2007. Cited hereafter as "Providing Land Tenure Security," *LTERA*.

Figure 40. The Author Shopping in Kabul. Housed in old shipping containers, shopkeepers' goods are secure. *Source: Author.*

ably minimize the number of evictions. Once approved by the municipality, it will halt forced evictions.[129]

A 2006 preliminary study of the LTERA project in District 7 was conducted by an Afghan NGO well-versed in the techniques and philosophy of community action planning, the Cooperation for the Reconstruction of Afghanistan (CRA). CRA identified the possibility of improved tenure security in terms of increased business activity and housing construction, especially where improvement in security of tenure was accompanied by community organization and the physical upgrading of the District's streets and drainage systems. Interviews with community leaders and residents also showed that people's perception of tenure security and general community conditions have improved significantly since the implementation of the project. In summary, the work done by the community is due, in large measure, to the organizational and guiding efforts of CRA and the financial support from USAID/EMG:[130]

---

129 "Providing Land Tenure Security," *LTERA.*

130 "Providing Land Tenure Security," *LTERA.*

Figure 41. Drainage is a Key Community Improvement. *Source: LTERA.*

More construction: 46 houses have either been reconstructed or extended in the pilot area since the implementation of the project. This represents 9% of all houses in the area. All but one of these houses are constructed of brick and concrete, a substantially greater investment than the usual mud construction.

More Businesses: The number of business activities has increased from 117 to 126, an increase of 7% since the last survey was undertaken ten months previously, in November 2005.

Increased Prices of Vacant Land: Although house prices appear to have stabilized and, in some instances, decreased in value, the price of vacant land has increased by as much as 50% since the project was implemented. There are fewer houses on the market than before the project started. There are fewer properties for rent, and rentals have increased by an average of 30% during the last year.

More Tenure Security: Thirty residents were interviewed regarding their knowledge and understanding of the LTERA upgrading effort. All but one felt more secure as a result of the project and believed that the area would eventually be formally incorporated into the City Plan. Three respondents noted that the mere fact that roads and drains had been constructed had resulted in improved perceptions of secure tenure.

Images of Title Deeds

Screen Prints of the Land Information System Linked to the Deeds Database

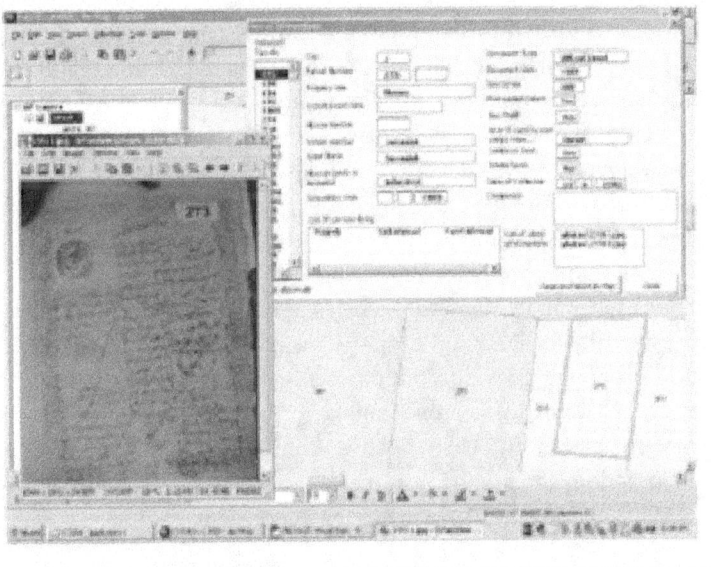

Figure 42. Archive Computerization and Digitization of Property Deeds. *Source: LTERA.*

Positive Impact on Community Development: The *shura* and community leaders involved with the property adjudication process reiterated their support for the project and confirmed that it had resulted in improved perceptions of security and increased economic activity.

By reducing fear of the forced eviction bulldozer, resolving disputes, demarcating plots, providing funds for community infrastructure upgrading, and actually enabling community development, each success, no matter how small, builds upon the other to provide security of tenure and upgrading of the settlement.

LTERA's Restoration of Legal Documentation in Afghan Registration Courts

When land disputes occur in Afghanistan, taking matters to the courts often only adds to the woes of returnees and others dispossessed of their land due to war, land-grabbing, or other avarice. Plagued by corruption, inefficiency, delays, and an inability to enforce decisions, the official justice system disappoints many Afghans, who understandably resort to customary dispute resolution methods.

In Afghanistan the Primary Courts in both urban and rural districts actually prepare title deeds when people come to the judges for this purpose. The Provincial Appeals Courts, located in the provincial capitals, maintain the archives of title deeds documenting the transfer of title according to procedures established by the Supreme Court. These archives, which contain all primary and provincial court documents and are maintained by the judiciary, are called *mahkzan*. But the author's visits to two Afghan *makhzan* revealed that "maintain" is perhaps too kind a word. During the Afghan civil war, *makhzan* suffered neglect and destruction, and were in generally poor condition. Many legal documents, including title deeds, were stolen, destroyed, and falsified, and fraudulent new title deeds were created for dubious property transactions. To restore confidence in the judicial system, it is essential to rehabilitate the legal archives and make them accessible to the public, especially for land and property disputes. LTERA's *Mahkzan* Rehabilitation Program's goal is to build on efforts started by previous USAID supported programs to improve land tenure security through the design and implementation of a cost-effective, transparent, accessible and simple deed preparation, and archiving and consulting system. The reorganization of the archives concentrates on the following objectives:[131]

82 |

- Sort the original legal documents to make them accessible to the public and the judiciary.
- Secure the legal documents that exist in the archives which can be used in the future to build a national Land Information System (LIS).
- Digitize and organize the digital records to improve the security of

---

[131] "Providing Land Tenure Security," *LTERA.*

Figure 43. Mahkzan Rehabilitation Photos: Before and After.
Source: LTERA.

storage of these documents, and to accelerate the delivery by the judiciary of certificates and duplicates of official title documents to the public.

By February 2007 more than 590,000 title deeds for immovable property had been re-organized and stored in dry and secure cabinets; 30,000 of these documents had been digitized.[132] The computerization of the archives and the digitization of title deeds not only preserve the documents, which were often in very poor condition, but also digital copies can replace hand-prepared duplicates. This makes it much more difficult to falsify existing

---

132 "Providing Land Tenure Security," *LTERA*.

title deeds or introduce new falsified property documentation. A transparent recording and archiving process with secure access to the legal information limits the possibility of corruption. The improvements in document storage and retrieval are real, but the system is not used by most people engaging in real estate transactions. In a city of over 3 million people, or at least 800,000 housing units, according to an LTERA employee, radio and newspaper public service announcements and the normal usage of courts for deed preparation have prompted an average of only 10-15 persons a day to visit the Kabul *Makhzan*. In most urban contexts, a land market of transactions averaging 20% of the properties each year would be a minimal expectation. In Kabul, that would mean perhaps 160,000 annual transactions, or about 600 per working day. The courts are clearly assisting with a small percentage of actual transactions. But even with a low rate of capture, the improvement in the archiving process is useful. Many Kabulites had given up hope that their deeds could be found, and are elated that legal deed copies can now be obtained. In some cases, the deed copies are used in the settlement of land disputes, and in others for proving property ownership to secure loans, and for inheritance clarifications.

Additionally, a national database has been created containing the indexing of 67,000 legal document registration books called *kundas*. The LTERA Project intends one day to be able to link property information in the *makhzan* with cadastral maps and databases maintained by the municipalities and government ministries. Linking these databases is essential to implement an integrated LIS. Once operational, the LIS will facilitate an efficient and cost-effective transfer of ownership of immovable property, support the development of a formal economy in Afghanistan, and provide greater tenure security to millions of Afghans.[133] The first steps toward these lofty goals have been taken, but much more needs to be done. LTERA is demonstrating that progress is better measured in small steps rather than stressing ambitious but unrealistic plans.

A Good Cadastre is a Great Achievement

"A good cadastre will be the greatest achievement in my civil code," said Napoleon, who 200 years ago wanted an end to costly and useless trials to resolve land disputes between neighbors. Napoleon sought to create a universal type of property right; its perennial representation would eliminate boundary disputes and facilitate uniform taxation. Cadastres, along with security of tenure, land policy, dispute resolution, are key tools in efforts to

---

133 "Providing Land Tenure Security," *LTERA*.

restore sound land administration to post-conflict nations. When used correctly, as shown in Angola, Cambodia, and Ethiopia, they can dutifully serve the local citizens rather than outside powers. In the case of Afghanistan, the various programs discussed show how promising registration of land-related rights can be to address the Afghan refugee crisis, Kabul's unwieldy urban growth, and to maintain peace on rural pasturelands. How might the results of community/participatory mapping, the plethora of legal, statutory, and customary land records, and competing post-conflict land claims be registered alongside formally held properties so that the power of GIS can be harnessed to visualize amicable solutions to land administration problems worldwide? This is the topic of Chapter 6.

CHAPTER 6:
Cadastre for Reconstruction and Stability: The Land Administration Domain Model

Land ownership, which springs from humanity's agricultural roots, predates recorded history. And as long as people have owned property, they have also sold it, bought it, and passed it on to their heirs. In antiquity to effect a transaction the parties involved would meet at the city gates in the presence of the community elders, or congregate in the marketplace in the presence of a government official, or assemble somewhere else in public and there agree upon their terms. The transaction may or may not have been written, depending upon local custom. But whether recorded in parchment, books, or peoples' memory, the transaction was public, and therefore considered legitimate.

This universal human practice is the basis for deeds, the written record of transfers of rights, ownership, or possession between parties. The word *deed*, which comes from the same root as the word *do*, implies an action, an activity. Although adequate in antiquity, and still practiced in many parts of the world, the deed in modern Western countries is insufficient to prove the legality of an exchange. After all, a perfectly legitimate deed may merely record how a thief sold stolen land. Competing, contradictory, or fraudulent deeds require adjudication. In response to a changing economic order, after the industrial revolution Western countries found a need to record the ownership of land parcels in a way that would make transactions easier to track and more readily available to government and financial institutions. This led to a shift to an absolute individual land parcel record of who owns what and where. Having clear title to a property gave financial institutions the ability to secure a loan against the property. This protected both the lender and the borrower. For the government, ownership was clear for taxation purposes, or in the case of eminent domain, the government knew who owned the property. This is how title-based land administration systems began in many Western countries.

Unlike a deed, which is a physical object, a title is conceptual. A title is a right a state gives to a certain person or persons recognizing the legitimate ownership or possession of a given property. There may be a document that acknowledges this title, but the title itself is the right, not the piece of paper. Whereas a deed always involves two parties and records a transaction at a certain time, a title, which must oftentimes be determined on the basis of deeds, merely declares who has what rights to what property.

Titles and Deeds in Cadastres

This somewhat oversimplified picture of the difference between deeds and titles helps explain competing models in land administration. Because of the stability of models of Western land administration, many foreign aid workers have attempted to establish in post-conflict societies systems based on titles, not deeds. Titles, unlike deeds, are well suited to computer databases and have no ambiguity about them. They are very familiar to the Western aid workers who are trying to rebuild the country. But there are problems with this ideal, as mentioned in the previous chapter. While such systems are slowly set up, a post-conflict society may degenerate further as one land dispute piles upon another. Titles have taken centuries to be established in Western civilization, yet this model of land administration would try to transform in a matter of months tribal societies and shattered, post-conflict nations without the foundational knowledge contained in a national cadastre. In fact, this is true for many countries in the world; only ten nations, mostly in Western Europe, report having total cadastral coverage. Developing countries such as Tanzania, Cambodia, and Namibia have cadastral coverage in 10, 18, and 60 percent of urban areas, and five, 10, and 20 percent of rural areas, respectively.[134]

Some of the specialists discussed in this book advocate moving from a title-based to a deeds-based model of land administration. A deeds-based model seeks to rebuild a post-conflict society by taking advantage of, and building upon, the integrity of centuries-old customs of recording land exchanges. The goal of a deeds-based model is to map the relationship between people and their land as quickly as possible—disputes, ambiguities, and all—and make this information available to local leaders, officials, judges, and citizens so the competing claims can be adjudicated and local social structures can be restored, without waiting for the central government to develop a corruption-free and competent public administration.

The same problem that plagues the title-based model also affects the deeds-based one. To map this terrain, one needs a cadastre, a record of who owns what, and who has what rights. How does one approach the

---

134 The University of Melbourne Department of Geomatics, *Cadastral Template* (Melbourne, Australia: University of Melbourne, 2007), URL: <http://www.cadastraltemplate.org/>, accessed 12 August 2007.

land issues in Afghanistan where cadastral coverage of populated places is virtually nonexistent?

Challenges in Cadastres

Most Western cadastres depend upon a title-based, centralized model of land administration. When imported into post-conflict societies, they prove ineffective or inadequate for a number of reasons. First, title-based cadastres adhere to strict database rules, so they are unable to handle ambiguous or vague boundaries common in post-conflict societies. A similar ambiguity occurs in cadastral descriptions of urban versus rural areas. Functioning cities require precise boundaries, with an accuracy of 10 centimeters or less. Rural areas have a greater tolerance for imprecision; in many cases an accuracy of 10 meters or less is sufficient. Unfortunately, many cadastres cannot merge different accuracies into a single data environment. By the year 2030 up to one third of the world's population will live in informal slums, so the requirement for urban-level accuracy is a major challenge.[135]

Title-based cadastres presume that land conflicts or ambiguities have been resolved, that deeds have been carefully examined to determine who legitimately holds the rights to the land. If two parties are in dispute, the property in question will not be legitimately registered in the cadastre until possibly years later, when the government is capable of adjudicating the claim. Meanwhile the cadastre remains incomplete, and the unreliability of the land records precludes planning, most investment, and infrastructure and environmental improvements. Title-based cadastres, which presume a black-and-white distinction between a property's legal owners and all others, generally cannot account for the distinction between formal and informal land tenure. Because cadastres are most effective when centralized, they are difficult to build. Logistics are a constant problem. How might survey reports be entered into a central database? Once there, if a discrepancy in the data is found, how is this finding conveyed to the regional survey, to have the issue revisited? How do local documents fit unambiguously the well-formed fields of the database, especially when local custom may not use the same distinctions presumed by the cadastral design?

One might logically think that cadastral information already serves as the foundation for objective comparisons of property regimes world-

---

135 Christiaan Lemmen, Clarissa Augustinus, Peter van Oosterom, and Paul van der Molen, "The Social Tenure Domain Model--Design of a First Draft Model," paper presented at the FIG Working Week 2007, 13-17 May 2007 (Hong Kong SAR, China), 3. Cited hereafter as Lemmen, Augustinus, van Oosterom, and van der Molen, 2007 conference paper.

wide, but this is illusory. There has never been an internationally accepted standard or method for evaluating land administration systems. Cadastres cannot be compared across borders. "Each land system reflects the unique cultural and social context of the country in which it operates."[136] Van der Molen cites this fact as one reason why title-based, conventional land administration systems have been unable to record rights and interests and thus manage informal settlements, customary tenure, and fluid, post-conflict situations.[137] The ability to measure, compare, and analyze the world's various cadastral systems is forthcoming. Rajabifard, Binns, Williamson, and Steudler have begun development of a cadastral template that can link the operational aspects of a country's land administration systems with its land policy. Side-by-side country comparisons and statistics, available on a public website at www.cadastraltemplate.org, are already useful for analysis. In 2006, for example, 39 nations' self-reports indicate that 67% have title-based cadastral systems, 24% deed-based, and the remaining 9% a mix of the two. It would seem that title-based cadastres are not as ubiquitous as one might presume.

One final issue that plagues the implementation of either title-based or deed-based cadastres is that various countries often describe parcels of land in their own unique national coordinate system, not in absolute latitude and longitude. There are attempts to make these various systems interchangeable. One of many new surveying reference systems under development worldwide is the African Geodetic Reference Frame (AFREF). The AFREF is a planned, uniform coordinate reference system for all 53 African countries to enhance the accuracy of multi-country, cross-border mapping and development projects.[138] Once the still-developing AFREF and similar initiatives are implemented, coordinates in existing reference systems can be transformed into new, standard coordinates independent of local origin or local datum.

Given these problems, could a cadastre be developed to apply to all countries and all situations? In the late 1990s Juerg Kaufmann and Daniel Steudler co-authored Cadastre 2014, a pioneering approach to model the cadastral domain based not on parcels, but on legal land objects. Pub-

---

136 Daniel Steudler, Abbas Rajabifard, and Ian P. Williamson, "Evaluation of Land Administration Systems," Land Use Policy 21 (2004): 4.

137 International Institute for Geo-Information Science and Earth Observation (ITC), "Land Administration: The Path Towards Tenure Security, Poverty Alleviation and Sustainable Development," paper presented at the ITC Lunstrum Conference: Spatial Information for Civil Society, 14-16 December 2005 (Enschede, The Netherlands), 66.

138 United Nations Economic Commission for Africa (UNECA), African Geodetic Reference Frame (AFREF), 2006, URL: <http://geoinfo.uneca.org/afref/>, accessed 12 September 2007.

lic rights and restrictions will be included as well as private ones. Cadastre 2014 is a fine starting point but is highly abstract, years away from any implementation. Nevertheless, Kaufmann supports the notion that a cadastre must depend more on deeds than titles in post-conflict society. He notes that a cadastre, with its traditional role of documenting land rights, restrictions, and responsibilities, can be viewed as a book-keeping or "accounting system" for land issues, ultimately supporting a post-conflict reconstruction period through the transition to sustainable development.[139]

Land Administration Domain Model (LADM)

Significant inventiveness on the part of Christiaan Lemmen, Clarissa Augustinus, Peter van Oosterom, and Paul van der Molen has resulted in the Land Administration Domain Model (LADM). Not yet an operational system, but a concept that international experts have been working on since 2002, the LADM is compelling because it makes explicit the various types of land rights, restrictions, or responsibilities. It is flexible enough to record land tenure types not based on the traditional cadastral parcel, i.e., customary, informal land rights such as occupancy, usufruct, lease, or traverse.

LADM may be the first step to an internationally recognized standard for a cadastre. It has garnered support from standardization and professional bodies such as the FIG, Open GIS Consortium (OGC), UN-HABITAT, and the Infrastructure for Spatial Information in Europe (EU-INSPIRE).[140] In May 2007 the International Standards Organization (ISO/TC211), the body responsible for determining all international standards, accepted the LADM as New Work Item Proposal (NWIP) 1954. A draft ISO standard is the next stage, one that may lead to the first internationally standardized cadastre.

The LADM has reduced the complex database models that underlie title-based cadastres to a simple principle: that a relationship (rights, socio-tenure) always exist between land (spatial objects) and people. No matter how messy or difficult the world's land disputes, nothing falls outside this basic principle. A person or group of persons have (or claim to have) certain rights to a given tract of land. The LADM translates these three categories into Unified Modeling Language (UML), a general purpose modeling

---

139 Juerg Kaufmann, "Future Cadastres: The Bookkeeping Systems for Land Administration Supporting Sustainable Development," paper presented at the 1st International Seminar on Cadastral System, Land Administration and Sustainable Development, 3-5 May 2000 (Bogota, Columbia). Cited hereafter as Kaufmann, 2000 conference paper.

140 Peter van Oosterom, Christiaan Lemmen, Tryggvi Ingvarsson, Paul van der Molen, Hendrik Ploeger, Wilko Quak, Jantien Stoter, and Jaap Zevenbergen, "The Core Cadastral Domain Model," *ScienceDirect 30, Computers, Environment and Urban Systems* (2006): 629.

language, to establish three classes for its cadastre: Person-Right-Spatial Object, in that order. The LADM enables registration and maintenance of "relationships between people and land irrespective of the nature of the country's jurisprudence; this ability offers opportunities for the integration of statutory, customary, and informal arrangements within conventional land administration systems."[141] For the first time in cadastral history the LADM enables the systemic recording of rights that are not title-based legal rights but claims that may need adjudication. It allows tremendous flexibility in describing the persons and places involved.

The LADM possesses the critical functionality to merge formal and informal land tenure systems, and urban and rural cadastres, into one data environment. LADM requires that spatial information be represented in multiple geodetic networks, which are systems to measure the earth's surface. Therefore, conversion from a local to a national, and, in the case of AFREF, to a continental reference system must be possible before LADM can become interoperable. These standards, as mentioned above, are already under development. In brief, the LADM promises the following features:[142]

- Formal and informal tenure systems can be held in one data environment.
- The computer-based system is reversible to and from a paper-based one.
- Spatial information can be represented in existing geodetic networks and in new spatial frameworks.
- Spatial data can be linked to other systems.
- The environment is distributed and decentralized, simultaneously processing on multiple geographically separated computers over a network, making it usable centrally and locally.
- Source data can be of disparate types, with different geospatial accuracies.
- Different tenures can be allowed to overlap.
- Places can be identified by a range of identifiers: geo-referenced parcels, unreferenced parcels, lines, points, and so forth.
- Conflicts can be recorded, women's access to land can be ensured, and highly complex relationships can be described.

---

141 Lemmen, Augustinus, van Oosterom, and van der Molen, 2007 conference paper, 7.
142 Lemmen, Augustinus, van Oosterom, and van der Molen, 2007 conference paper, 12.

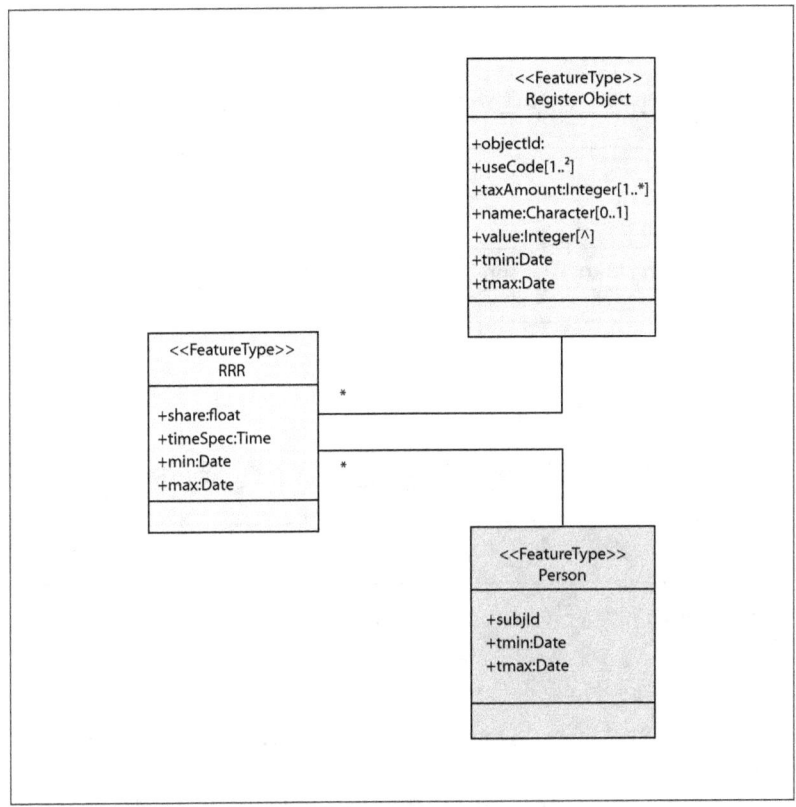

Figure 44. The Central Premise of the Land Administration Domain Model.
Source: Christiaan Lemmen, et. al. http://www.fig.net/pub/fig2006/papers/ ts12/ts12_02_lemmen_vanoosterom_0605.pdf. RRR = Right, Restriction, Responsibility.

LADM Components

As mentioned above, LADM depends upon three classes of objects: persons, rights, and spatial units. Figure 44 illustrates the central premise of the LADM, that a land-related right, or better stated, a socio-tenure relationship (a term based on the 2003 UN-Habitat Continuum of Rights), always exists between land and people. In Figure 44, yellow marks social tenure relations; green, persons; and blue, spatial units.

Two of these classes—rights (or informal social land tenure relationships) and persons—are administrative or legal. The other class, spatial unit, is geographical. The difference is important, for it reflects the two pillars of all land administrations. On one side is the administrative or legal aspect. Who has the property? Do they own or possess it, or do they have

| 93

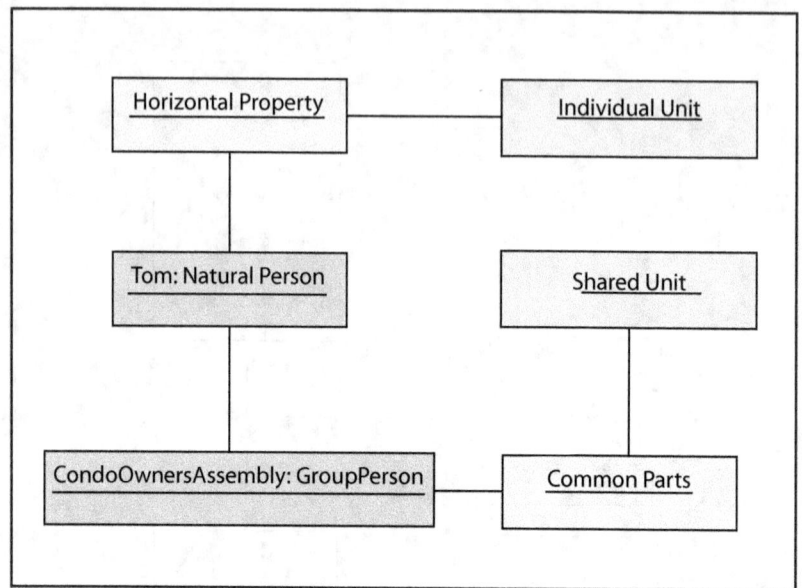

Figure 45. Horizontal Property Objects. *Source: Modified by author from Hespanha et al.*

other rights? What taxes do they owe? On the other side is the geographical requirement. Exactly what is the land? What are its borders? What immovable structures are on the land? Thus, at its core, the LADM reflects the two aspects common to all land administration systems.

LADM Modeling

To illustrate LADM flexibility, it may help to look at two dimensions of landholding that have proved difficult for traditional cadastres to handle: complex spaces and changes in time.

The worldwide rural to urban migration has sparked a significant increase in multi-unit dwellings, such as condominiums. Figure 45 shows how LADM proposes to treat individual units within a multi-unit building. Individual units in such "horizontal property" relate to a specific natural person, Tom, through the Right of Horizontal Property. To fully characterize Horizontal Property, however, common areas of the building, represented by the spatial object Shared Unit, are related to the group of persons holding Horizontal Property Rights on the Building, that is, the "Condo Owners Assembly," a Group Person, through a

Common Parts Right.[143] Thus, in Figure 45, rights (in yellow) mediate between spatial objects (light blue) and persons (in green). In this way LADM can accurately reflect a complex arrangement made between an individual and group in an equally complex building.

Now let's add to this scenario the dimension of time. In recent years time-share units, typically in resort areas, have become attractive to own. These units are often condominiums, but the right of use is fixed, for example, to the same one or two weeks each year. This type of recurring use right is best described in a cadastre with four dimensional (4D) representation, so as to correctly situate the object of the right both in the space (3D) and in time.[144] Table 2 below shows how a fourth dimension expands the range of possible rights, restrictions, and responsibilities to be recorded in a cadastre.

Sharing Type	Right	Restriction/Responsibility
No share in space No share in time	Individual property ownership	Homeowners association covenants/restrictions apply
No share in space	Time sharing	Pay annual maintenance fee
Share in time	Succession usufruct	Maintain property's condition for subsequent use
Share in space No share in time	Co-owned property	Auto-limiting rights require majority of owners' vote to change landscape contract

Table 2. *Source: modified by author from Hespanha et. al.*

LADM: The Future of Cadastre

LADM links spatial data from very different systems. In the past this linking has been very problematic for land information, in part because of the database structure. To link disparate data, however, LADM is less a database than a word processor. Anything can be put into the document, as long as it records all evidence relevant to a property and the rights various people claim on it. Thus, LADM is especially suited to recording deeds.

Land information systems should serve decision makers at national, regional and local level with the emphasis on decentralized decision making. This is the basic concept behind the LADM: to produce and provide (1)

---

143 João P. Hespanha, Mónica Jardim, Jesper Paasch, and Jaap Zevenbergen, "Modelling Legal and Administrative Cadastral Domain — Implementing into Portuguese Legal Framework," (2007), 26. Cited hereafter as Hespanha, Jardim, Paasch, and Zevenbergen, "Modelling." Unpublished manuscript provided to author.

144 Hespanha, Jardim, Paasch, and Zevenbergen, "Modelling," 12.

land registration (the administrative/legal component) and (2) geo-referenced cadastral mapping (the spatial component) for land administration in a decentralized environment. The model will allow better vertical coordination, between "bottom up" local/community interests and "top down" information and policy guidance. National development policies can be harmonized with local programs.[145] Thus, LADM facilitates the rehabilitation of both local and central governance.

The LADM fulfills the criteria outlined by Kaufmann to be reliable, systematic/complete, appropriate to needs and laws, adaptable to development, public, and transparent.[146] And whereas Cadastre 2014 is a generic, abstract set of guidelines, the LADM is a real system under real development. It is pragmatic because unique socio-tenure relationships can be represented to reflect the realities on the ground.

It may be objected that the LADM cannot represent all possible cases for one area of the world, or that the categories it describes for one country may need to change for the next. But this is LADM's strength, not its weakness. The classes in LADM are expandable. The system is being designed so that additional attributes, operators, associations, and perhaps even complete new classes can be added for a specific country or region.[147] For example, Tryggvi Már Ingvarsson and his colleagues suggest how the LADM can reflect the natural features of the Icelandic landscape, which are in constant motion and change in extent and shape.[148]

> In the CCDM [an earlier name of the LADM], fuzzy boundaries may be employed and applied in such circumstances. The CCDM [LADM] supports this concept using history attributes, but an approach using specially defined boundaries would be more appropriate. One way to adapt the CCDM [LADM] to Icelandic requirements would be by conceptually defining a number of new boundary types. Boundaries the veracity of which have not been established, [and] designated general boundaries can be identified only by further research. Fixed boundaries have been surveyed according to requirements as defined in laws and regulations. Dynamic boundaries are boundaries between public and private lands subject to change over long periods, such as coastline change, glacial movement or due to individual events such as volcanic activity. These

145 Lemmen, Augustinus, van Oosterom, and van der Molen, 2007 conference paper, 13.

146 Kaufmann, 2000 conference paper, 3.

147 Lemmen, Augustinus, van Oosterom, and van der Molen, 2007 conference paper, 8.

148 Tryggvi Már Ingvarsson, Tom Barry, and Margrét Hauksdóttir, "Reform of Icelandic Cadastre," *GIM International, The Global Magazine for Geomatics* 21, no. 3 (2007), URL: <http://www.gim-international.com/issues/articles/id867-Reform_of_Icelandic_Cadastre.html>, accessed 27 September 2007.

boundaries are considered fixed at each period of time. Fuzzy boundaries are those subject to more attenuated periods of change on a smaller scale; riverbeds are an example. Fuzzy boundaries can also be used to indicate areas of conflicting interests.

The LADM aspires to be everything that civilian land administrators and civil-military planners want to address regarding land issues of post-conflict societies. It merits close attention by NATO, the U.S. State and Defense Departments, and USAID or other entities tasked with bringing about stabilization because it could be an important breakthrough tool for aiding countries with weak or totally absent land administration.

CHAPTER 7:
Applied Geography as a Mainstay of U.S. Foreign Policy

In 1999, following a vote for independence from Indonesia, widespread violence in East Timor destroyed countless buildings and homes. Abandoned properties invited illegal occupation by the 150,000 people, or 15% of the population, who became IDPs. In early 2006, renewed violence resulted in more property destruction, a new wave of displaced persons, and further confusion of the earlier property restitution claims already underway. A 2006 USAID Conflict Vulnerability Assessment in East Timor found that "the inadequacy of mechanisms to resolve disputes over land and property rights cause[d] land tenure insecurity and can encourage [a] resort to violence."[149] The UNHCR has long advocated a four-phase return process: repatriation, reintegration, rehabilitation, and reconstruction. With the end of the Cold War, repatriation became more realistic and attractive as a durable solution to the international refugee problem; the UNHCR even declared the 1990s as "the Decade of Repatriation."[150]

A rights-based approach to resettlement and repatriation is now in vogue. The Pinheiro Principles, noted in Chapter 2, declared that refugees and IDPs should be guaranteed a variety of restitution rights. According to the Principles, displaced persons may either return to their land or instead claim financial compensation, should they wish not to return. East Timor's descent into renewed violence in 2006 underscores the fact that human rights pronouncements from Brussels and Geneva are as ineffectual as was the international community's response to the 1999 East Timorese civil war. A rights-based approach has severe limitations. The Pinheiro Principles do not instruct reconstruction and stability (R&S) practitioners on the ground what to do concerning land tenure and property rights (LTPR). The Principles do not say who should pay restitution or how various claims should be adjudicated, to separate the fraudulent from

---

149 Cynthia Brady and David G. Timberman, "The Crisis in Timor-Leste: Causes, Consequences and Options for Conflict Management and Mitigation," report for the USAID (Washington, DC: USAID, 2006).

150 United Nations High Commission on Refugees (UNHCR), *The State of the World's Refugees 2006 - Chapter 6, Rethinking Durable Solutions: The Search for Durable Solutions (2006)*, 2006, URL: <http://www.unhcr.org/cgi-bin/texis/vtx/publ/opendoc.htm?tbl=PUBL&id=4444d3ca28>, accessed 25 September 2007.

genuine. The rights-based approach often amounts merely to a well-meaning platitude. It envisions an ideal but says nothing about how to achieve it.

The international community should recognize that a rights-based approach alone is insufficient, and that a rule-of-law approach to LTPR must also be embraced. A rule-of-law approach acknowledges that in a conflict or disaster the international community's most urgent responsibilities pertain to public security and humanitarian assistance. No less important (but seemingly easily forgotten) are the mandates to restore legal, educational, and legislative institutions. These priorities, discussed in Chapter 2, must include land administration at the forefront. The rule-of-law approach invests immediately in the restitution of central and local institutions, to implement changes that are merely wished for in rights-based approaches. Noted experts De Soto, Foley, and Rubin advocate a rule-of-law approach, both for the sake of short-term stability and for longer-term economic development.

The 2006 USAID report mentioned above prompted the government of East Timor (GOTL) to establish a national land registration and titling system. The initiative is praiseworthy, but how will it be implemented? Will the international community help GOTL with a rights-based or a rule-of-law approach? The GOTL will require substantial technical assistance, concerted human resources, institutional capacity building, and, more than anything else, time to achieve these objectives. The UN-HABITAT *Handbook for Planning Immediate Measures from Emergency to Reconstruction* soberly reminds practitioners that long after the media, emergency services personnel and stability forces pull out of a country, post-conflict land management "is dependent on political will and a determination to build effective systems— including technical and governance—over long periods. As a rule of thumb, it takes about 25 years to build such a system."[151]

East Timor, a nation of only one million people, requires both immediate and long-term commitments for its needs in land administration. R&S practitioners there must implement a viable land administration system now. Foreign aid agencies and donors must take a long view of the matter. How might land administration receive a much higher priority in whole-of-government and whole-of-alliance R&S doctrine, human, and technical resources? How should civilian and military personnel be trained to deploy to collapsed states, knowing that land administration, unlike short-term emergency aid distribution, takes

---

[151] Clarissa Augustinus and Dan Lewis, *Handbook for Planning Immediate Measures from Emergency to Reconstruction (Peer-Reviewed First Draft)*, ed. Paul van der Molen, Japp Zevenbergen, and Thierry Naudin (Nairobi, Kenya: UN-HABITAT Disaster, Post-Conflict, and Safety Section and the Land and Tenure Section, 2004), 126. Cited hereafter as Augustinus and Lewis, *Handbook*.

years, perhaps decades, to institutionalize? This chapter presents recommendations on how U.S. government agencies should adapt and change to be prepared to address future land crises, both in the short and long term.

The Early Phase of Addressing Land Crises: The Role of the Military

George Boguslawski was deployed to Afghanistan with the U.S. Army Corps of Engineers Contingency Real Estate Support Team (CREST). His experience shows that an intervening U.S. military force can trigger conflict by inadvertently creating a land market and that one of the first needs in a country is a repository for recorded land-related rights and interests, rights both substantiated and claimed. Boguslawski explains:

> A group of Afghans leased their land, previously of negligible worth, to the U.S. Army based on the ownership documents they had provided. Since ownership disputes are common, our leases stipulate that a competing ownership claim stops payment until the dispute is resolved. Months later another man claimed partial ownership of the same land. We stopped paying on the lease and informed the first party that payments will resume as soon as that party got a decision from the court. These folks swore that the other guy had no right to the land. They even brought a village elder to lend credibility to their argument. When I explained that the matter must be settled in court, they told me that it was not possible because the other guy is "al-Qaeda" and refuses to go near courts or law enforcement. It is common for parties in disputes around Kabul to accuse each other of being al-Qaeda or Taliban. When telephoned, the alleged al-Qaeda man unhesitatingly agreed to come to the base the next day. He brought court papers indicating that he had filed suit over ownership of the property. He turned out to be related to members of the first party.

> Weeks later, the first party resorted to chicanery in order to gain an audience with me; that party showed base security a document with a seal on it and told security that it was a court document. Security telephoned me that the group had brought a court document with them. This "court document" was written in poor English and was covered with the thumbprints of the group members. The seal was actually to verify that the thumbprints belonged to the individuals named in the document. The "court document" was nothing more than a letter from the group demanding that I pay them. Shortly after they realized that I was not going to decide the issue of ownership, the parties settled out of court by

Figure 46. Military "First-Responders" to a natural disaster are greeted in Nicaragua. *Source: Department of Defense.*

signing a supplemental lease agreement; we then paid the rent that had been withheld.[152]

With increasing frequency, the first responders to post-disaster and post-conflict crises are the U.S. and allied armed forces, trained to deal with any number of contingencies. Former U.S. Marine Corps Commandant Charles Krulak coined the term "three-block war" to describe three missions: combat, peace enforcement, and humanitarian, that the U.S. military could be expected to execute within a three-block radius of a given urban center. Lieutenant Colonel Steven Fleming, a geography professor at the U.S. Military Academy, relates that resolving land conflicts is indispensable for operations other than war, so that for two of the three missions of the three-block war concept it is important. This is in striking contrast to wars of bygone eras. Military planners in WWII were not concerned with property ownership when planning a battle, aside from making sure they minimized destruction to selected cultural locations. Even in the recent fighting in Iraq, Fleming notes that "From a military position, warfighting, e.g., 'the March to Baghdad,' does not concern itself much with land ownership. However, post-conflict nation-building and reconstruction inherently involve mass movements of people. Therefore, knowledge of land ownership is central to the success of

102 |

---

152 George Boguslawski, U.S. Army Corp of Engineers, phone interview by the author, 2 August 2007.

Figure 47. A Symposium Sponsored by the U.S. Naval Postgraduate School's Center for Stabilization and Reconstruction Studies. *Source: NPS.*

those missions."[153] For military or civilian responders, early assessment of the state of post-conflict land records, of land institutions, and of land prob- | 103 lems is an integral part of restoring peace and stability. Round-the-clock food, water, medical, shelter, and other emergency aid distribution often eclipses the need to conduct these assessments. A lack of public clamor about land issues invites further postponements.

---

[153] Steven Fleming, Professor of Geography at the U.S. Military Academy, e-mail interview by the author, 10 August 2007.

Citing his experience in Liberia, Jon Unruh cautions R&S specialists not to be fooled: in postwar countries a surge of land tenure problems tend to surface three to five years after the fighting ceases. "This is because in the immediate postwar lull, people are upgrading livelihoods in rudimentary ways. But, at about three to five years, continued upgrading needs a property rights system and it is then that the problems emerge. While social unrest connected to land and property issues is unlikely while UNMIL [United Nations Mission in Liberia] has a large presence in the country, at some point the peacekeeping forces will be stepped down and the rule of law needs to step up."[154] Naturally, the ideal time to head off a post-conflict land crisis, as occurred in East Timor, is to anticipate it and, soon upon arrival in a country, develop a cadastral framework, years in advance of the inevitable problems.

While military forces are often the first responders to world crises, most would gladly limit their role to providing security so that other entities can execute their own vital missions. In a perfect world, NGOs deliver humanitarian aid; intergovernmental bodies such as the UNHCR resettle refugees. It may seem that involvement in local land matters, something normally relegated to civilian agencies, is not in the interest of the military. But in reality, the military's involvement in recording early land disputes enhances, not hinders, its military mission. Joseph Nye, former Chair of the U.S. National Intelligence Council, and Deputy Under Secretary of State for Security Assistance, Science and Technology, coined the term "soft power" as the ability to get what you want through attraction rather than coercion.[155] Nye lamented that only in academic circles, in Europe, even in China and India, but not in the United States, has soft power entered into political debate, and that the global attractiveness of the U.S. has been squandered by a singular hard power (military) approach to foreign policy.[156] Current and future conflicts, labeled Fourth Generation Warfare, Irregular Warfare, Insurgency, or Asymmetric Wars, require a great deal of soft power to achieve an agreed-upon end state: "the imposition of law and order to generate regional stability, development, peace, and effective sovereignty."[157] To meet these future challenges, Dr. Max Manwaring of the U.S. Army Strategic Studies Institute theorizes that a national executive-level management

154 Jon Unruh, *Postwar Land Tenure in Liberia: Lessons Learned from Other Post-Conflict Countries* (2007), 3.

155 Joseph S. Nye, *Soft Power: The Means to Success in World Politics*, 1st ed. (New York: Public Affairs, 2004), x.

156 Joseph S. Nye, "After Rumsfeld, a Good Time to Focus on Soft Power," *Daily Star* (Beirut, Lebanon), 11 November 2006.

157 Max G. Manwaring, "Defense, Development, and Diplomacy (3D): Canadian and U.S. Military Perspectives," paper presented at the Defense, Development, and Diplomacy (3D): Canadian and U.S. Military Perspectives, 21-23 June 2006 (Kingston, Ontario, Canada), 3. Cited hereafter as Manwaring, 2006 conference paper.

structure and an international coordinating entity are essential for ensuring vertical and horizontal unity of effort.

Dealing with these kinds of national and global threats involves the entire population of affected countries, as well as large numbers of civilian and military national and international governmental and nongovernmental organizations and agencies — and sub-national, indigenous actors. As a result, a viable unity of effort is required to coordinate the many multidimensional, multi-organizational, and multilateral/multinational activities necessary to play in a given security arena.[158]

The Pentagon has already anticipated this new role by incorporating stability operations into the war colleges' curricula, thereby preparing regional combatant commanders for their expanded role.

Some Western nations are increasing the allocation and training of military forces for peacekeeping, peace enforcement, and stability, known collectively as "military operations other than war." Canada, for example, has implemented a Defense, Development, and Diplomacy (3D) approach "in developing a new external conflict and internal catastrophe/disaster paradigm in which traditional military and police organizations continue to play major roles, but are closely coordinated with all the other instruments of power under the control of the civil authority. The 3-D concept is rapidly growing into a broader and more effective strategic whole-of-government and grand-strategy whole-of-alliance paradigm."[159]

The Next Phase in Land Crises: Civil-Military Cooperation

These new initiatives in the military emphasize collaboration with relief and development organizations. Recent post-conflict scenarios have at times forced military forces to assume the unconventional (and perhaps uncomfortable) roles of humanitarian aid providers and nation-builders. Although the military is there, ready and able to assist, these roles ultimately are best served by neutral civilians. Military and civilian organizations must learn how to cooperate, especially how to effect the transfer of the military's short-term responsibilities to civilian specialists. Ideally this hand-off would occur a month or two following the end of hostilities, and the military would play a supporting role until its presence is no longer required. In recent operations a smooth transfer of those responsibilities has been difficult to achieve.

---

158 Manwaring, 2006 conference paper, 3.
159 Manwaring, 2006 conference paper, 1.

To understand why the military-to-civilian hand-off of nation building tasks is problematic, consider the experience of Deborah Alexander. In spring 2002, USAID sent Alexander to Afghanistan to build relations with the U.S. military and prepare the way for agency experts to aid in that country's reconstruction. "Alexander would land at a clandestine airfield and then hitch a ride with a passing United Nations convoy to get to a military base. Once there, she would find the civil-affairs unit: 'Hi, I'm from the government and I'm here to help.' Civil-affairs soldiers were always happy to see her, even if they didn't know she was coming, and they would quickly brief her on the local water, agricultural, and health challenges. She made friends and learned about the needs to be filled by the USAID experts —who arrived 18 months later."[160] Alexander explains:

> It takes a while to get them recruited, trained, and out there. Unlike the military, neither USAID nor State has a standing reserve of civilian experts ready to deploy. They can send a few people quickly, but for such substantial operations as those in Afghanistan or Iraq, both have to recruit staff, write and sign contracts, and conduct training — a time-consuming process for which the situation on the ground can't wait. In an ideal world, the military would be a supporting partner to a broader civilian-led operation. But that's challenged by the very real fact that the civilian agencies are under-resourced. Even if they started building capacity today, it would still take a long time. As a result, in the short term, the burden falls on the military.[161]

Clearly, transition and cooperation need to be better coordinated. The U.S. Congress is now pursuing reforms that would better integrate the departments of Defense and State and the U.S. Agency for International Development. First, the National Security Presidential Directive (NSPD) 44, issued in December 2005, promotes the security of the United States through improved coordination, planning, and implementation of reconstruction and stabilization assistance for foreign states and regions of, in, or in transition from, conflict or civil strife. NSPD-44 provides some much-needed vitality to the newly created State Department Office of the Coordinator for Reconstruction and Stabilization (S/CRS). Regarding policy, NSPD-44 states that "the United States should work with other countries and organizations to anticipate state failure, avoid it whenever possible, and respond quickly and effectively when necessary and appropriate to

---

160 Corine Hegland, "Pentagon, State Struggle to Define Nation-Building Roles," *Government Executive*, 30 April 2007, URL: <http://www.govexec.com/mailbagDetails.cfm?aid=36760>, accessed 5 May 2007. Cited hereafter as Hegland, "Pentagon, State Struggle."

161 Hegland, "Pentagon, State Struggle."

promote peace, security, development, democratic practices, market economies, and the rule of law."[162] In another significant reform, the National Security Council in 2007 approved models for interagency cooperation for the next country collapse. It also agreed on an idea to create a National Security Education Consortium to provide joint education and training for civilians and the military.[163]

Addressing Land Crises in the Long Term: Building Land Administration Expertise

Outside of a few Civil Affairs and legal specialists, neither active duty nor reserve military members can realistically develop cadastre and land administration expertise. The long-term needs of a post-conflict country are best served by deployable civilian experts who are well trained and equipped with the resources needed for lengthy stays. Unfortunately, this is one of the greatest deficiencies in the fledging U.S. R&S apparatus. Zimmermann identifies the worldwide dearth of human resources and cadastral frameworks to meet future crises:

> International experts and national professionals are confronted with a huge task that requires specific professional knowledge in terms of building an enabling framework, tackle critical governance issues, institutional re-engineering, situation-specific sequencing and prioritizing and the design of a long term program in the land sector.... The international community is short of governance responsive "post-conflict" land experts and can not yet sufficiently meet the challenge on the ground.[164]

The international community is unprepared to address the scale of the problems posed by land crises. And the U.S. is the least prepared, despite having the most resources. Unlike in Europe and Canada, in the U.S. the disciplines of land administration and geomatics (engineering-surveying spatial data management) are scarcely known. The author visited officials of the S/CRS and USAID officials and contractors working to improve land tenure and property rights work (LTPR) in Afghanistan. The paucity of American know-how was evident—and waning further as the few remaining USG LTPR experts approach retirement age. The USAID relies largely on private consulting firms who acquire their experience from short-term contracts. The con-

---

162 The White House, NSPD-44 Management of Interagency Efforts Concerning Reconstruction and Stability (Washington, DC: 2005).

163 Hegland, "Pentagon, State Struggle."

164 Zimmermann, 2006 conference paper, 12.

tracted employees, with increasing frequency non-U.S. citizens, do not always have a sophisticated, broad-based understanding of property rights issues. And because USAID employs few LTPR experts, on-the-ground oversight of contractor performance by at least one USG official is increasingly rare.

This situation has arisen partly due to underestimating the role land administration plays in R&S, and partly due to changes in government practices that have not been sufficiently scrutinized. The idealistic 1960s image of American government employees, Peace Corps volunteers, and academics engaged in exchanges and international development has long since disappeared. Stanfield outlines the changing nature of American foreign aid over the last 60 years, and, from his observations in Afghanistan, concludes that something has gone terribly wrong:

> The years following World War II witnessed the emergence of the United Nations, the dissolution of many aspects of colonialism, and the emphasis on state investments in core industries and infrastructure to move countries into the "development" stream. The assistance of developed countries in this process was often government-to-government, or in the form of people-to-people programs (such as the Peace Corps and exchange programs), or involved voluntary organizations which shifted their post war humanitarian relief efforts to development investments, and even got universities involved, which encouraged their faculty and students to undertake international development programs.[165]

In recent years, a fundamental shift has occurred in assistance to developing countries. What was once handled by the USG is now managed by for-profit corporations. Instead of government or intergovernmental employees conducting the work, or, in several cases, even overseeing the work, organizations such as the USAID, but also the European Union, Inter-American Development Bank, Asian Development Bank and the World Bank, have contracted with corporations to deliver development assistance to countries in need. "Since 2000, the value of Federal contracts signed by all U.S. agencies each year has more than doubled to reach $412 billion dollars."[166] Stanfield notes the unfortunate effects and unintended consequences when foreign aid reflects not the face of a donor country, but that of a company. "I have witnessed in Afghanistan the rapid loss of Afghan support for the international development assistance

---

165 J. David Stanfield, "Land Administration in (Post) Conflict Conditions: The Case of Afghanistan," paper presented at the World Bank Conference on Land Policies & Legal Empowerment of the Poor, 2-3 November 2006 (Washington, DC), 14.

166 Georgie Anne Geyer, "'Outsourcing' Is Not the Answer to Our Foreign Policy Woes," 23 August 2007, *Yahoo! News*, URL: <http://news.yahoo.com/s/ucgg/outsourcingisnottheanswertoourforeignpolicywoes>, accessed 29 August 2007.

programs being run by foreign corporations. Afghans deeply resent seeing the often ostentatious and counter-productive results of such programs."[167]

Afghanistan is the proving ground for American R&S in the 21st century. Others familiar with what is happening there echo Stanfield's sentiments. First, the incentive for millions of refugees to return to Afghanistan was the billions of dollars in promised foreign aid, which was perceived by returnees as a hedge against homelessness and unemployment. "Unfortunately, the Government of Afghanistan (GoA) did not directly receive the aid which donor countries had promised to give for the reconstruction. Instead, a number of NGOs and individuals in key positions received everything."[168] Next, Afghan Finance Minister Anwarul Haq Ahady occasioned some uneasiness in a 2007 U.S. Congressional forum on Afghanistan when he too suggested that foreign aid should be routed through the GoA, and not directly to the NGOs. He decried the lack of any discussion on the "output" of foreign aid and pointed out that projects not routed through the GoA were being done at a much higher cost. Ahady's insight was supported by two other eminent experts who participated in the the panel discussions, Barnett Rubin, Director of Studies and Senior Fellow, Centre for International Cooperation, and Marvin Weinbaum, Scholar in Residence, Middle East Institute. Referring to an instance where nearly $100 million was transferred to the bank account of a consultant in Washington to carry out a project in Afghanistan, Rubin said, "This may sound too harsh. But if we give the money directly through the Afghan government, USAID would be much more effective...Money in Afghanistan is not being used effectively; funding is being dispersed, but is not delivered."[169] The previous year Rubin wrote, "more than seventy-five percent of all aid to Afghanistan funds projects [were] directly implemented or contracted by donors. This mode of delivery, although initially inevitable, is ultimately self-defeating. If prolonged, it undermines—rather than builds—the state"[170] Lastly, a former NGO operative, 17 years in Afghanistan with Norway Church Aid, Mohammad Ehsan Zia, now Afghanistan's Minister of Rural Rehabilitation and Development, asks: "Do non-governmental agencies really want Afghanistan to get off its knees, no longer reliant on the international humanitarians bountiful? It is a loaded question. After all, that would put them out of business, redundant to Afghanistan's emerging—as hoped—self-

---

167 J. David Stanfield, *Privatization of International Development Assistance Stirs Resentment in Afghanistan* (Mount Horeb, WI: Terra Institute, Ltd., 2006), 1. Cited hereafter as Stanfield, *Privatization*.

168 ANIS, "Expulsion of Afghan Refugees: A Wave of Poverty and Unemployment," *ANIS (Companion) State-Run Daily Newspaper* (Kabul, Afghanistan), 3 March 2007.

169 Lalit K. Jha, "Minister's Call for Aid Effectiveness Upsets U.S. Official," *Pajhwok Afghan News*, 21 April 2007, URL: <http://www.afghanistannewscenter.com/news/2007/april/apr212007.html#19>, accessed 14 September 2007.

170 Rubin and Hamidzada, "From Bonn to London," 23.

determination... NGOs seem very much in competition with the government. Why? Because business as usual suits them very well."[171]

Behind all these changes in foreign aid lies the simple notion that government is less efficient than private companies, which, in competition with each other for contracts, develop agile, cost-effective structures. Thus, goes the logic, taxpayers' money would be spent more effectively through contracted firms. But in reconstructing Afghanistan, flaws in the principle have been exposed. Businesses are in business to turn a profit; NGOs, too, must justify their continued existence. Public service is not the priority. Stanfield, who understands the negative effects of corporate privatization of development assistance, fostering paternalism, undermining the legitimacy of the GoA, and slowing the country's reconstruction, also suggests a way out of the conundrum:

> This model is also defective from an effectiveness perspective. The corporate managers of development assistance under this privatized corporate model determine "what is better to do" about development problems by calculating "what is better for their foreign corporate profits," and not what is better for the countries which should be benefiting from development assistance...A drastic re-thinking of the structure of foreign assistance is urgently necessary. One direction of this re-thinking is for development assistance to build the capacity for its own administration in the local governmental and non-profit sectors, including local universities.[172]

For this to happen, two major developments must occur in U.S. R&S efforts. First, the United States must recognize that R&S is inherently a government function and designate and resource branches of government to specialize in R&S. Second, the USG should begin to aggressively train and maintain a cadre of R&S expertise: civilian and military, full- and part-time (reservists), with a robust emphasis placed on land administration skills.

---

[171] Rosie DiManno, "Aid Groups Wearing out Welcome," *The Star* (Toronto, Ontario, Canada), 23 April 2007.

[172] Stanfield, Privatization, 2.

Mobilizing Government to Respond to Land Crises

To project American soft power throughout the world, the State Department must take the lead. In 2004 then-Secretary of State Colin Powell created the S/CRS, but it has been only partially resourced. For example, in 2004 the Office requested $350 million to build a Civilian Reserve Corps, similar to the Pentagon's military reserve, which would deploy civilians with critical nation-building skills. Congress remitted $7 million. The Pentagon came to the rescue; Chairman of the Joint Chiefs of Staff, General Peter Pace, offered $100 million out of Defense's 2006 budget.[173] In 2007, the Office asked for $25 million to create a smaller Civilian Reserve Corps, which Congress again denied. Oddly, "President Bush mentioned the [Civilian Reserve] Corps in his 2007 State of the Union speech, but his fiscal 2008 budget request to Congress the following month included no money to pay for it. Political experts who are watching this process say that the Corps is the key, and that its creation comes close to a make-or-break deal for a partnership between the civilian and military wings of the government. It would represent the first real investment in desperately needed civilian capacity."[174] The Special Inspector General for Iraq's reconstruction, Stuart Bowen, "urged the [USG] agencies to focus on clearly delineating authority and procedures in multi-agency operations and singled out the S/CRS as an appropriate leader on interagency efforts, and urged Congress to fully fund it."[175]

What would this Civilian Reserve Corps look like? S/CRS can look to a partner country, Norway, for a model of how to recruit, train, and deploy "stand-by" civilians to troubled areas of the world. Established in 1991, the Norwegian Refugee Council's (NRC) stand-by force of 650 is larger than the initial 500-person Civilian Reserve Corps planned by S/CRS. NRC emergency stand-by forces aim to strengthen the UN capacity in emergency situations and have become one of the most important suppliers of personnel to the UN and to other humanitarian organizations. Nearly one-third of the NRC stand-by force is assigned to Special Forces for Human Rights, Democratization, and Disaster Relief or NORDEM. The proposed U.S. Civilian Reserve Corps could adopt a model similar to NORDEM. See Appendix D for the tentative skill mix of the Civilian Reserve Corps, which includes three positions for cadastre/land administration experts. This may be a start, but realistically it should be ten times that number to begin a U.S. LTPR community of prac-

---

173 Hegland, "Pentagon, State Struggle."

174 Hegland, "Pentagon, State Struggle."

175 Jenny Mandel, "Reconstruction IG Urges Interagency Coordination," *Government Executive,* 22 March 2007, URL: <http://www.governmentexecutive.com/dailyfed/0307/032207ml. htm>, accessed 12 April 2007.

tice. Some NORDEM characteristics to consider in establishing a U.S. Civilian Reserve Corps include:[176]

- NORDEM Stand-by force is a co-operative project of the Norwegian Centre for Human Rights and the Norwegian Refugee Council (NRC). The Norwegian Centre for Human Rights is professionally responsible for assessments, reports, training, briefing, and debriefing. The NRC carries overall administrative responsibility, including budgeting, accounting, practical arrangements for deployment, and security in the field. Recruitment is a shared responsibility.

- NORDEM Stand-by force now includes 250 members within the above-mentioned categories ready to take on six-month international assignments on short notice.

- Recruitment takes place annually through advertisements in national and regional newspapers, written applications, and group interviews.

- All newly recruited members are required to attend the NORDEM Basic Training Course. This is a six-day course that consists of three components: first, education focusing on international and regional mechanisms for the protection of human rights, and the UN's mandate, structure, and human rights operations; second, skills training in the field of human rights and democratization work; third, practical aspects of international fieldwork. Basic training is organized once a year and is seen as a prerequisite for international assignments.

- Prior to a given assignment secondees (participants) are briefed about the assignment and the situation in the country of assignment. The secondees have already received relevant written documentation and briefing materials.

- After the completion of an assignment, debriefings are organized and the secondees submit a written report. These are regularly published, both in print and in web editions as *NORDEM Report*.

Training in Land Administration

Where will the needed land administration experts come from? In the S/CRS, personnel will require a unique skill set to execute the immediate tasks in any post-conflict arena:[177]

---

[176] The University of Oslo, the Norwegian Refugee Council, and the Norwegian Centre for Human Rights, *"Norwegian Resource Bank for Democracy and Human Rights (NORDEM)—A Brief Presentation,"* (Oslo, Norway: 18 May 2005), URL: <http://www.humanrights.uio.no/english/research/programmes/nordem/>, accessed 15 September 2007.

[177] Augustinus and Lewis, *Handbook*, 9.

- Retrieving and assessing land records.
- Determining the degree of validity of the land records.
- Getting the registry and cadastral services running again.
- Launching mechanisms for the resolution of land disputes.
- Informing the population about the above.

"These tasks require expertise in land records from the twin points of view of land registries and cadastral registries or maps. More specifically, such expertise ranges from legal-administrative to survey-technical."[178] Coincidently, these are the two components that compose the LADM. Astonishingly, training in the first component is not readily found in U.S. institutions of higher education (the Land Tenure Center at the University of Wisconsin—Madison no longer offers coursework, but focuses on policy analysis). The only aspect of the legal-administrative side of cadastre that most Americans are familiar with are real estate valuation and property taxes, and that due only to homeowner experience. Thus to be effective in land-related R&S operations, USG personnel will need skills difficult to acquire in the U.S., but obtainable abroad.

Several European programs, at reasonable tuition rates and with English as the language of instruction, offer specific training in land administration with field research conducted in developing countries.

- The International Institute for Geo-information Science and Earth Observation (ITC) is a United Nations University. The campus in Enschede, the Netherlands, offers 3-week to 18-month certificate, diploma, and Master of Science degree programs in Land Administration. See *www.itc.nl/education/courses/landadministration.aspx*

- The Technical University of Munich, Germany, offers an International Master's Program in Land Management and Land Tenure as well as short-term training. Three semesters are spent on campus and conducting field research. The thesis can then be written from the student's home country. See *http://www.landentwicklung-muenchen.de/master/index.html*

- The Swedish International Development Cooperation Agency (Sida) offers advanced international training in urban land administration in two phases. A four-week training session in Sweden is followed by distance education from the student's home country. Months later a second phase is conducted in a city of the developing world. See *www.swedesurvey.se/files/pdf/Invitation%20Brochure.pdf*

| 113

---

178 Augustinus and Lewis, *Handbook*, 24.

A number of foreign institutions offer higher education in geomatics and other fields with a land-tenure emphasis.

- University of Glasgow, U.K. offers a Master of Science in Geoinformation Technology and Cartography, in 6 month modules. See *www.ges.gla.ac.uk:443/degrees/postgraduate/courses/MScGTC*

- Sweden's Royal Institute of Technology, the Unit of Real Estate Planning and Land Law, with a focus on property law and property economics, offers a Master's programme in Land Management. See *www.infra.kth.se/FV/lm/new/index.php?&M=1&MENU=1*

- The University of Melbourne, Australia, offers degrees in geomatics. See *www.geom.unimelb.edu.au/*

- The Institute of Social Science, the Hague, the Netherlands, offers short courses and graduate degrees in various international development topics, to include LTPR. See *www.iss.nl/*

- The University of New Brunswick, Canada, offers a Geodesy and Geomatics Masters degree in Land Administration/Land Information Management. See *http://gge.unb.ca/HomePage.php3*

Although higher education in the U.S. has few comparable programs (see Appendix E for the syllabus of Dr. Grenville Barnes' graduate course in Land Tenure and Administration at the University of Florida), there are distinct signs of such courses becoming available. In March 2007, legislation was introduced to "establish a 5,000-person undergraduate academy, on par with the nation's [five] military academies, to inject prestige into public institutions and highlight the importance of public service."[179] Soon thereafter, Kathy Newcomer, president of the National Association of Schools of Public Affairs and Administration, responded with a less expensive alternative, a "virtual academy" that utilizes existing universities' resources. The debate is likely to continue for years as to whether it makes sense to offer an elite civilian counterpart to young people who want to serve their country outside of the military.[180] The further question remains: if a civilian service academy were established, would there be a department or faculty of Foreign Policy/Foreign Assistance? Existing curricular resources could lay the foundation for new programs, or they could be immediately implemented by programs of those universities that are already preparing future civil servants. The new USAID three-day short course, Land Tenure, Property Rights, and Natural Resource Management-Constraints and

---

[179] Brittany R. Ballendstedt, "Universities Propose Alternative to Public Service Academy," *Government Executive*, 21 May 2007, URL: <http://www.governmentexecutive.com/dailyfed/0507/052107b2.htm>, accessed 4 April 2007. Cited hereafter as Ballendstedt, "Universities Propose Alternative."

[180] Ballendstedt, "Universities Propose Alternative."

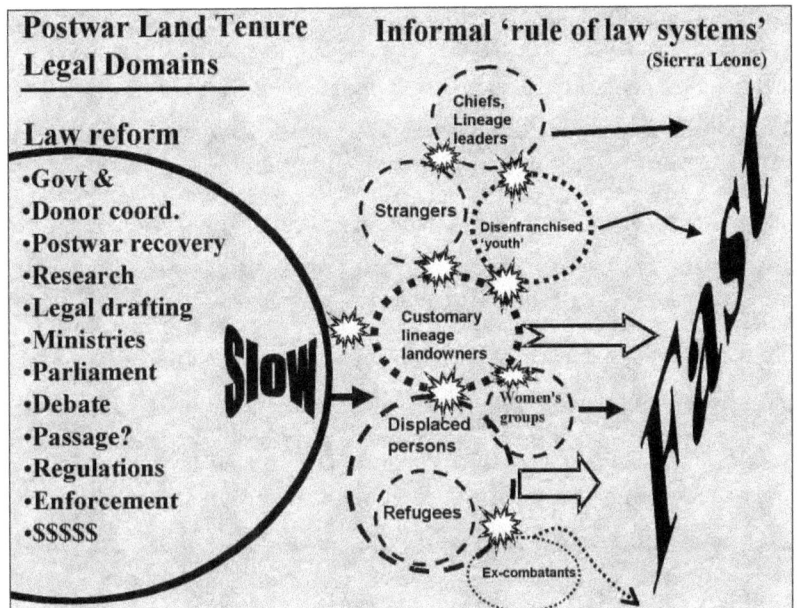

Figure 48. A Post-Conflict Land Issues Training Scenario. What to do when informal land tenure systems emerge much faster than formal institutions?
Source: Courtesy of Dr. Jon Unruh, 2007.

Best Practices,[181] and the spectrum of land tenure manuals and studies[182] published by the Food and Agriculture Organization of the UN, could easily form the basis for a series of one-semester-hour seminars. Within a Foreign Policy/ Foreign Assistance department, might sequenced LTPR-related courses be molded into a curriculum? Quite possibly, but those courses must first be developed.

Perhaps the time needed to establish a civilian service academy, or a virtual university equivalent, will allow the most-experienced R&S operator, NATO, to compile the lessons it has learned and develop much-needed R&S training standards. Despite more than a decade of experience with R&S operations, NATO has yet to incorporate R&S into its defense planning process and force requirements planning. Aware of this deficiency, the Atlantic Council of the United States published a timely policy paper in 2006, *How Should NATO Handle Stabilisation Operations and Reconstruction Efforts?* One key recommendation from the paper is the establishment of an explicit NATO R&S mission, which would, in turn, stimulate the development of appropriate planning

---

181 USAID, "Land Tenure and Property Rights Vol. 1," *Framework* (2007).

182 Food and Agriculture Organization of the United Nations (FAO), *Access to Rural Land and Land Administration after Violent Conflicts* 8, *FAO Land Tenure Series* (Rome: FAO Publishing Management Services, 2005).

and organizational changes. Another recommendation is for NATO to improve its R&S planning and coordination with civilian organizations: "The Alliance should build familiarity, trust, and habits of cooperation with relevant non-military institutions prior to operational deployment."[183] Regarding civil-military cooperation and training, many an alliance member government looks to NATO for leadership. Especially by inviting civilian participation and observation in R&S exercises, NATO is uniquely positioned to "lead an effort to develop uniform standards for all military forces participating in R&S operations, and to assist in designing the necessary training.... Also, by sharing the process for creating military standards, NATO may be able to contribute to a similar effort to establish standards for civilians engaged in R&S."[184]

Certainly, NATO's lessons will play a central part in new initiatives in the training of LTPR specialists. Possibly more important to the success of these ventures is the reinstatement of geography as a pillar of the American education system. If American children are not learning geography in primary and secondary schools, they are unlikely to understand spatial problems or to have an interest in geography or related disciplines in either college or their professional lives.

In August 2007 President Bush signed the bipartisan America COMPETES (Creating Opportunities to Meaningfully Promote Excellence in Technology, Education, and Science) Act. The Act helps to "bring back geography" by adding the social sciences to the disciplines considered a priority at the National Science Foundation (NSF). The NSF's Geography and Regional Science Program falls under the Social, Behavioral, and Economic (SBE) Sciences Directorate, and the COMPETES Act specifically targets the social sciences as a priority.[185] This federal initiative coincides with a renewed interest in human geography at the high school level. The Association of American Geographers (AAG) reports:

> Advanced Placement (AP) Human Geography test rates for 2006 are up 49% from 2005. This year 20,003 students sat for the exam which measures performance in college-level AP human geography courses offered in high schools...The AP Human Geography course is structured around a syllabus that meets college standards and follows an outline that parallels college course content, including themes and models such as globalization, cultural diffusion, and central place theory...Recent world events combined with the development of

---

183 C. Richard Nelson, *How Should NATO Handle Stabilisation Operations and Reconstruction Efforts?* policy paper (Washington, DC: The Atlantic Council of the United States, 2006), 21. Cited hereafter as Nelson, *Stabilisation Operations*.

184 Nelson, *Stabilisation Operations*, 21.

185 John Wertman, "AAG Washington Monitor," *AAG Newsletter* 42, no. 8 (2007): 5.

geographic technologies turned around a decline in geography in the United States during the latter half of the twentieth century. A holdover from this decline though was difficulty in recruiting majors, due to the lack of geography knowledge of incoming freshman...AP Human Geography has opened up a new world for over 50,000 students in the past six years, and we expect an increasing number of these students to continue their geography education in college.[186]

AAG President Kavita Pandit desires more geography majors to study abroad. "As a discipline we still have not embraced study abroad as a key component of geography undergraduate education. Yet there are compelling reasons for us to do so, not the least of which is that study abroad vitally connects to two long-standing traditions in geography: area studies and field work."[187] Indeed, in 2003-04, fewer than two percent of enrolled U.S. students studied overseas. Pandit pitches the benefits of studying geography abroad by describing the exciting field work and by noting the importance of the global service learning projects. For faculty members, she touts the opportunities to include students in their field research. And such opportunities abound: a 2007 NSF study revealed that 69% of geography departments in the U.S. offer some kind of international field course for their students.[188] Pandit concludes, "study abroad programs can, therefore, reconnect geographers with our field-based tradition and help students to develop into truly well-rounded geographical scholars."[189] The Bowman Expeditions discussed earlier in Chapter 4 ideally lend themselves to this purpose.

Overall, the growth of geography in secondary and higher education suggests that America has the potential to become once again, as in Woodrow Wilson's day, the envy of the world and a story of success in foreign affairs. The international community's efforts in post-conflict nation building are continually hampered in much the same way as the noble ideals of the UN elude implementation. The rights-based approach to repatriation and resettlement of refugees and IDPs must give way to a rule-of-law approach if results are to be achieved and maintained. For the part of the U.S., civilian and military agencies must embrace R&S partnership roles that ensure a speedy, effective recovery in post-conflict societies. Now is an ideal time to change the course of foreign policy, when geography is on the verge of a return to the center of American education and culture.

---

186 Donald Ziegler and Barbara Hildebrandt, "Advanced Placement (AP) Human Geography Testing Surges," *AAG Newsletter* 41, no. 11 (2006): 4.

187 Kavita Pandit, "Integrating Study Abroad into Geography Higher Education," *AAG Newsletter* 41, no. 11 (2006): 3. Cited hereafter as Pandit, "Integrating Study Abroad."

188 Patricia Solis, *Results from Advancing Academe: A Multidimensional Investigation of Geography in the Americas (AAMIGA)*, unpublished report to the National Science Foundation (Arlington, VA: NSF, 2007).

189 Pandit, "Integrating Study Abroad," 3.

CHAPTER 8:
Conclusion

According to U.S. Government Accountability Office (GAO) figures, the conflicts in Afghanistan and Iraq have been costing the United States about $70 billion per year, and by 2007, over 4,000 Americans had died in the conflicts. The loss of life and resources has placed an economic and emotional drain on Americans. A strategy that can stabilize the Afghan and Iraqi governments and allow the United States to depart would be beneficial to the American people. Creating stable, legitimate governments in these and other volatile states is a goal of American foreign policy.

Though ending conflicts will require many forms of action, one method that can help to create stability is to place more emphasis on political, economic, legal, and educational aid. One very specific aspect of this aid is to have selected U.S. government (USG) agencies focus on land tenure and property rights (LTPR) in the developing world. This would, possibly more than any other kind of foreign aid, transform a volatile state into a capable one. Capable, that is, of maintaining stability by resisting and deterring the violent extremism of non-state actors through the strength of its civil society.

On January 8, 2001, USAID and the Woodrow Wilson International Center for Scholars jointly sponsored a conference in Washington, DC titled *The Role of Foreign Assistance in Conflict Prevention*. Eighty experts from USAID, the State Department, the National Intelligence Council, Congressional staff, academic institutions, the business community, and non-profit organizations gathered together "to shape a new vision for foreign assistance by developing a long-term strategy keyed to conflict prevention and building capable societies."[190] The terrorist attacks of September 11, 2001, followed by the ongoing military operations in Afghanistan and Iraq, threaten to make conflict prevention a quixotic ideal in foreign policy circles. Yet the accuracy with which the 80 conference participants presaged, prior to September 11, 2001, how U.S. foreign assistance in the 21st century must change is most remarkable. The conference's six themes were:[191]

---

190 USAID and the Woodrow Wilson International Center for Scholars, "The Role of Foreign Assistance in Conflict Prevention," conference report (Washington, DC: 8 January 2001), URL: <http://www.usaid.gov/pubs/confprev/>, accessed 6 September 2007. Cited hereafter as USAID, "The Role of Foreign Assistance."

191 USAID, "The Role of Foreign Assistance."

- Recognize the importance of conflict prevention.
- Expand the definition of national security.
- Construct capable states.
- Build local capacity.
- Engage multiple actors.
- Develop better mechanisms for collaboration.

This book, by offering a rationale and a model for registering the human terrain, a key, singular application of American soft power, gives much-needed impetus to the 2001 conference's purpose: to re-examine "traditional concepts of national security to embrace a broader spectrum of political, economic, and social issues that will have a direct impact on the core needs of the American people."[192] The following recommendations enhance the conference's *leitmotif* by specifying a whole-of-government effort to strengthen LTPR in volatile areas of the world instrumental to U.S. national security.

- **Recognize the importance of *land* in conflict prevention.** As should be clear from this book, land issues are often at the epicenter of violent conflict around the world, a dimension at times lost on U.S. policymakers. For half a century American institutions of secondary and higher education have not emphasized geography and have all but ignored land issues. The post-Cold War period has been marked by few foreign policy, and fewer post-conflict nation-building, successes. The USG must recognize anew the importance of registering the human terrain. A land registration system, with its dispute resolution component, can prevent or lessen conflict by bringing simmering land and property disputes into the public forum and recording the resulting local adjudications.

- **Expand the definition of national security *to include security of land tenure.*** Under the feudal king described in Chapter 3, holding land, not necessarily owning it, enabled the rise of stable nation-states that understood that peace is more conducive to prosperity than is war. By the same token policymakers must understand that a nation will never be secure as long as its citizens' LTPR are not, and the insecurity of other nations erodes U.S. national security.

  Specifically, commit to win the peace as much as to win the war by aiding other countries to build land information systems and the human resources capacity to maintain them. Where a cadastral system is in use, rule of law is evident, and, according to International Federation of Surveyors (FIG) President Stig Enemark, "the system

---

192 USAID, "The Role of Foreign Assistance."

acts as the backbone of society."[193] This change is optimal to the projection of U.S. soft power.

- **Construct states *capable of administering land.*** Capable states are characterized by:[194]
    - ° Representative governance based on rule of law.
    - ° Market economic activity.
    - ° A thriving civil society.
    - ° Security, well being, and justice available to all citizens.
    - ° The ability to manage internal and external affairs peacefully.

Chapter 3 suggested that registering multiple rights and interests in land and property is the missing foundation to six years of reconstruction and stability (R&S) efforts in Afghanistan. Afghanistan's overlapping and poor governance of land matters is not an isolated occurrence. Most developing countries have far too many institutions involved in land matters. Where land information exists, it is housed not in a single system but in several government ministries, which makes access exceedingly difficult. Without proper standardization and agreements, a multipurpose, interoperable cadastral system cannot be realized.

The infusion of technical assistance in the cooperative Afghan Mapping Initiative is an example of how a government's capacity to register its human terrain is improved. A Basic Education and Cooperative Agreement signed in June 2007 by the National Geospatial-Intelligence Agency (NGA) and the Afghan Geodetic and Cartographic Head Office (AGCHO) outlines how NGA will provide hardware and technical assistance to AGCHO: training in using GIS software, archiving geospatial data, standardizing geographic names, creating boundary databases, and in geodetic surveying and management topics.

- **Build local capacity *in resolving land conflict.*** Stanfield noted that | 121 in rural Afghanistan "a local consensus exists about the rights people have to land, and that local definition is the starting point to define

---

193 International Institute for Geo-Information Science and Earth Observation ITC, "Land Administration: The Path Towards Tenure Security, Poverty Alleviation and Sustainable Development," paper presented at the ITC Lunstrum Conference: Spatial Information for Civil Society, 14-16 December 2005 (Enschede, The Netherlands), 17.

194 Stanfield, "Community Recording."

rights and rules."[195] The Rural Lands Administration Project, the International Land Coalition, and the first Bowman Expedition were three cited examples of soft power wielded by a government foreign aid agency, an NGO, and academia that facilitated local capacity and spread goodwill. Exciting new tools are being developed that facilitate these works. The Land Administration Domain Model (LADM) is the first viable cadastral model to incorporate informal, customary land claims and records into a comprehensive land registry so that the institutions of civil society, even the *shuras* and *jirgas* of Afghan society, can apply the rule of law. The LADM's distributed data environment offers communities the opportunity to record land rights and interests and resolve disputes themselves. When the central government develops the capacity for a regional or national land information system, local communities can be confident that their land records will integrate into the larger system.

- **Engage multiple actors** *in land-related R&S.* Intervening military forces must be prepared to retrieve and assess land records, and in some cases, begin determining the degree of their validity. Within 30 to 60 days, a hand-off of land administration tasks from military to deployed R&S civilian personnel must occur. The transition from post-conflict R&S to long-term sustainable development will require years, if not decades, and thus a host of civilian specialists (USG employees, contractors, NGOs, academics and students) to work the legal issues and, as in the case of post-conflict Cambodia from Chapter 5, train nationals in cadastral surveying and land administration.

- **Develop better mechanisms for collaboration.** National Security Presidential Directive 44, mandating civil-military cooperation in R&S, is in early development. But without resources, this directive's ideals cannot be realized: the State Department Office of the Coordinator for Reconstruction and Stabilization (S/CRS) must be fully funded immediately and assume its whole-of-government R&S coordinating role. The number of property law/cadastre experts within S/CRS's Civilian Reserve Corps must increase tenfold from three to 30.

---

195 USAID, "The Role of Foreign Assistance."

The LADM is the first viable land administration model for whole-of-government and whole-of-alliance use. For multinational R&S efforts and for multi-component organizations, such as the UN and NATO, cadastral interoperability is absolutely essential. The LADM should be populated, tested, and further developed for suitability in a variety of post-conflict and post-disaster environments. For this to occur, land administration must become an essential USG civilian occupation and a community of practice must be established.

In the key area of training, this book goes beyond the themes of the conference. Much of the world's current LTPR expertise resides in Europe, and those resources need to be tapped immediately. USG agencies should aggressively recruit from, and offer training and related experiences abroad to their current employees to build geographic expertise, especially in land administration.

For example, agencies should offer recruitment bonuses to graduates of the International Institute for Geo-information Science and Earth Observation (ITC), the Technical University of Munich, and participants in Swedish International Development Cooperation Agency (Sida)-style experiential programs who enter USG service. Many USG agencies offer long term graduate school training to competitively selected employees. The parochial mindset that limits long-term training to classrooms in U.S. institutions must end. Agencies should send their R&S personnel to foreign institutions for long-term training in LTPR and on field-based geographic research and Bowman-type expeditions abroad. Just as U.S. colleges and universities responded to a government's need for homeland security degree and certificate programs following the terrorist attacks of September 11, 2001, once the need is articulated, LTPR education programs will likewise be established in the U.S. A whole-of-government emphasis on LTPR enables a new direction in U.S. foreign policy to focus on conflict prevention and the construction of capable states. With an agile, well-trained, highly coordinated set of USG agencies aiding other nations to register the human terrain, American foreign policy can contribute to building a stable world where more people enjoy the benefits of secure property rights.

ACRONYMS

Acronym	Term	First Chap. w/ term
3-D	Defense, Development, and Diplomacy	7
AAG	Association of American Geographers	4
ADB	Asian Development Bank	5
AFREF	African Geodetic Reference Frame	6
AGCHO	Afghan Geodesy and Cartography Head Office	P*
AGS	American Geographical Society	4
AP	Advanced Placement	7
AREU	Afghanistan Research and Evaluation Unit	3
CARE	Cooperative for Assistance and Relief Everywhere	4
COHRE	The Centre on Housing Rights and Evictions	2
COMPETES	Creating Opportunities to Meaningfully Promote Excellence in Technology, Education, and Science	7
CRA	Cooperation for the Reconstruction of Afghanistan	5
CREST	Contingency Real Estate Support Team	7
DfID	U.K. Department for International Development	5
DNI	Director of National Intelligence	2
DW	Development Workshop	5
EMG	Emerging Markets Group	5
ESRI	Environmental Systems Research Institute, Inc.	4
EU	European Union	7
EU-INSPIRE	Infrastructure for Spatial Information in Europe	6
FAO	Food and Agriculture Organization of the United Nations	5
FARC	Revolutionary Armed Forces of Colombia	4
FIG	International Federation of Surveyors	P*,1
*In third column P is for Preface.		

ACRONYMS (Continued)

Acronym	Term	First Chap. w/ term
GGE	Geodesy and Geomatics	7
GoA	Government of Afghanistan	3
GOTL	Government of East Timor	7
GPS	Global Positioning System	4
GTZ	Gesellschaft für Technische Zusammenarbeit	2
HLP	Housing, Land, and Property	3
IC	Intelligence Community	4
ICLA	Information Counseling and Legal Aid	5
IDB	Inter-American Development Bank	7
IDP	Internally Displaced Persons	1
ILC	International Land Coalition	4
ISO	International Standards Organization	6
ITC	International Institute of Geo-Information Science and Earth Observation	P*
KCLIS	Kosovo Cadastre and Land Information System	5
KU	University of Kansas	4
LADM	Land Administration Domain Model	1
LAS	Land Administration System	5
LIS	Land Information System	5
LMAP	Land Management and Administration Project	5
LTERA	Land Titling and Economic Restructuring of Afghanistan	5
LTPR	Land Tenure and Property Rights	P*
MNF-I	Multi-National Force-Iraq	4
NATO	North Atlantic Treaty Organization	1
NGA	National Geospatial-Intelligence Agency	P*
NGO	Non-Government Organization	1
NORDEM	Norwegian Special Forces for Human Rights, Democratization, and Disaster Relief	7
*In third column P is for Preface.		

Acronym	Term	First Chap. w/ term
NRC	Norwegian Refugee Council	5
NSPD	National Security Presidential Directive	1
NWIP	New Work Item Proposal	6
OAS	Organization of American States	1
ODNI	Office of the Director of National Intelligence	P*
OGC	Open GIS Consortium	6
PROCEDE	Program for Certification of Ejidal Rights and Titling of parcels	4
PRT	Provincial Reconstruction Team	3
R&S	Reconstruction and Stability	1
RLAP	Rural Lands Administration Project	5
S/CRS	State Department Office of the Coordinator for Reconstruction and Stabilization	7
SBE	Social, Behavioral, and Economic	7
Sida	Swedish International Development Cooperation Agency	7
TFR	Total Fertility Rate	3
U.S.	United States	3
UML	Unified Modeling Language	6
UN	United Nations	1,2
UNDP	United Nations Development Program	2
UNECE	United Nations Economic Commission for Europe	2
UN-HABITAT	United Nations Human Settlement Program	5
UNHCR	United Nations High Commission on Refugees	2
UNMIL	United Nations Mission in Liberia	7
USAID	U.S. Agency for International Development	P*,1
USG	United States Government	P*,1
WB	World Bank	7
WWII	World War II	4
*In third column P is for Preface.		

APPENDIX A:
México Indígena Project Cycle

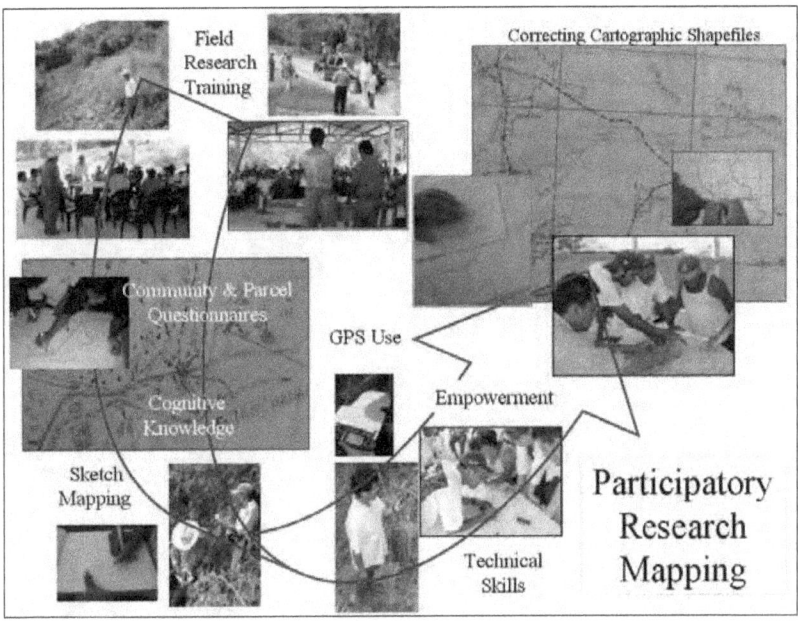

Source: México Indígena website, http://web.ku.edu/~mexind/methods.htm.

APPENDIX B:
AGCHO Cadastral Survey Forms

FORM 6A FOR THE TABULATION OF PARCEL INFORMATION

Survey Form 6A
Page:

The Land Survey and Statistics Department
List of Probable Land Ownership
Based on Inventory Survey (*Survey Aajel*)

Date:

Tax Collection Location: Field: Woluswali: Province: Eco-Geographical Grade:

Number of Parcel	Sheet Number	Area in Jirib and Grade	The probable owner name & ID number	Father's Name	Tax payer and Father's Name	Type of Transaction and Document	Water Source	Introduced By	Name & Signature of Neighbors

We hereby certify that the above mentioned survey is based on our information and correctly written. The boundary of each parcel is registered according to the agreement and introduction of the owners and neighbors.

Name & Signature:

Head of Village: Amlak Staff: Chief of Surveying Team: Land Classification Staff: Remarks of Chief of Surveying Group:

APPENDIX B (Continued)
(Revised Form 6)

Survey Form 6B
Date of Survey:
Page:

Council of Ministers
Afghan Geodesy and Cartography Head Office
Cadastral Survey Department
Cadastral Survey Regional Directorate
List of Land Ownership

Province:
Woluswali - Alaqadari:
Tax collection location:
Village-Subterranean canal:

Number of Parcel	Sheet Number	Area in Jirib	Owner Identification			Tax Payer Identification			Garden	Cadastral Land Grade						Non-Agricultural Land		Remarks
			Name	ID Number	F. Name	Name	Father's Name		Garden	1st Quality	Average	Poor	Poorer	Rainfed	Area	Type	

Prepared By:

Checked By:

The relevant authorities Remarks and Signature:

APPENDIX C:
Engineer Safar's Three-Level Strategy

Engineer Safar suggested a three-level strategy for establishing a land administration system in Afghanistan:

1. Improve the technical capacity for mapping property

   o Introduce the teaching of modern information and communication strategies in technical institutes. The FIG could be asked to design the content of the new curricula.

   o Provide equipment and working tools for training with these technologies and encourage their acquisition by the private and public sectors

   o Digitize the existing maps and records of the Cadastre and Amlak archives. A unified and compatible technical effort can begin following an analysis of the archived information

2. Decentralization of Property Records Administration

The present practice is for transaction documents to be validated locally by village elders and leaders. Copies of these documents are kept by the parties to the transaction. The basic idea is to add to this present practice in two ways:

   o Create the capability to record and archive the transaction documents at the local level in villages or combinations of villages, where local elders and respected people can oversee and verify the continuous accuracy of the locally archived property information. Documents so recorded would be given in law a preferential legal status over documents not recorded.

   o Provide the village shuras with satellite images with sufficient precision to show boundaries of villages and sub units of villages in the larger villages. Through agreements with the Judiciary, these "tax units" would be referenced in the transaction deeds showing the approximate location of the properties involved in the transactions.

3. Build a national technical and financial property information infrastructure as support for this local property information infrastructure.

   o Establish National Land Agency (NLA) for land administration as distinct from State Land Management which would be a separate administrative unit.

a) Land Registration and Cadastre Support Unit (Provide support to the local recording offices, to monitor their operations, and provide archive services if desired by the local recording offices.)

    i. Rural

    ii. Urban

    iii. Combine Cadastral Survey and Amlak property information of Cadastre and Amlak into land registration information system for support of local recording offices.

b) Property Tax Unit for supporting the local assessment and collection of property taxes, urban and rural land parcels.

c) Training Unit for Land Registration and Cadastre and Property Tax Units

d) Legal Unit for Drafting Legislation and Organizational Structure

e) Judiciary Liaison Unit to build capacity of Judiciary to incorporate cadastral information, at a minimum the Tax Unit location of the properties, into deeds and provide copies to NLA.

f) Land Inventory Unit, which will work with priority areas to estimate the approximate areas of different types of land: irrigated, orchard, cultivated rain fed, pasture, forest.

- Establish priority Provinces and Woluswalies (rural districts of Afghanistan)
- Acquire satellite images of these priority areas
- In consultations with village elders and leaders, establish boundaries of Tax Units [villages and combinations of settlements] and establish claims to pasture and forest land within these units.
- Prepare cadastral maps and updated Amlak ledgers of property owners for Tax Unit for those villages and woluswalies which want to participate in community legitimization of rights to agricultural, pasture and forest lands.
- Prepare forms and procedures for community property legitimization program.
- Establish Support Units for assisting communities conducting community property legitimization programs.

APPENDIX D:
500-Person Civilian
Reserve Corps Skill Mix

Composition of the first 500

SKILLSET	YEAR 1
SECURITY/RULE OF LAW	350
Justice Sector/Rule of Law Coordination	9
CJS planner/Coordinator (system analysis)	3
Independent CJS inspections and complaints specialists	4
Justice Sector Public Information Specialists	2
Policing	38
Police/Police Advisers	228
Crime Prevention Function	0
Command and Control [Including senior ministry advisor(s)]	9
Criminal Investigations Function	21
Emergency Services Experts (SWAT, Civil Disorder)	12
Evidence Collection Experts	2
Evidence Analysis Experts	2
Information Management Function	3
Internal Investigations Function	3
Police Legal Advisor Function	
Maintenance Function	6
Narcotic Interdiction/Investigation Function	6
Operational Communications Function	6
Patrol Function (including some border patrol)/mentor	120
Personnel Administration Function	3
Planning Function	3
Public Information/Outreach Function	3
Purchasing and Supply Function	3

Records Function	3
Traffic Function	7
Training Function	12
Weapons Registration Experts	2
Forensic Laboratory Function	2
Explosive Incident Response	
Firearms Proliferation and Interdiction	
Counter-terrorism Function	
Special Investigative Function	
Intelligence Based Development	
Border Integrity	**10**
Border Patrol (enforcement) advisors	6
Customs (regulatory) advisors	2
Immigration (regulator) advisors	2
Corrections	**28**
Senior Ministry Advisors (organizations, system, capacity experts)	3
Physical security expert and Prisoner Classification	3
Logistical expert	2
Records/legal expert (sentence calculation, court hearing schedule, access to legal counsel, treatment of prison) standards)	2
Medical expert	2
Facilities, planning, construction	3
Security threat group/Riot Control	3
Finance/human resources training	2
Training director	2
Transportation administrator	2
Security/prisoner management supervisor	4

Justice System	75
Prosecutorial Function	9
Prosecutors (general practice- likely local and state backgrounds)	5
Senior Ministry Advisers	4
CJS integration specialists (see top)	
Specialized Prosecutorial Functions	15
Money laundering	3
Terror Related-Financing, etc	3
Organized Crime	3
Trafficking in Persons	2
Narcotics interdiction and investigation	2
Anti-corruption experts (criminal and civil penalties)	2
Court Functions	29
Magistrates (trial and investigative)	3
Judges (trial and appellate)	11
Senior Ministry Advisor	3
Court Administrators (incl Senior organizational court experts)	4
Adjudication training experts, etc	2
Judicial Security/Witness Protection	1
Personnel Security/ Judges	1
Facility Security-Courthouses	1
Mediation/Alt dispute resolution experts	3
Defense	4
Defense/Advocacy attorneys	4
War Crimes	6
War Crimes Forensic Experts	2
Remediation/Reparations experts	2
Human Rights/Anti-Corruption Experts (10) under DG	

War Crimes/Crimes against humanity/genocide	2
Other Rule of Law	**12**
Bar Association Advisors	2
Comparative law specialists (incl. traditional systems of justice, alternate dispute resolution)	3
Legislative/Code drafters/Constitutional	3
Training curriculum	2
Trial advocacy skills trainers	2
ECONOMIC AND SOCIAL WELL BEING	**100**
Essential Services/Business Development	**50**
DDR Expert	3
Property Law/Cadastre Expert	3
Commercial Law Expert	2
Business Development Adviser (Private Sector Development)	3
Senior Ag Adviser	3
Senior Ag Economist	3
Rural Development Advisor	3
Social Services	
Finance	
Microcredit Expert	
Public Utilities	8
Transportation	6
Water and Sanitation	6
Telecommunications	
Civil/Construction Engineering	10
Natural Resource Management Advisor	
Monetary/Economic Stability	**11**
Monetary Policy Advisor	4

Banking Advisor	5
Tax Policy Advisor	
Fiscal Policy Advisor	
Budget Formulation/Execution Advisor	2
Health	**27**
Public Health/Med Reconstruction Team Leader	1
Public Health/Med Reconstruction Deputy and Donor Coordinator	1
Public health service delivery	5
Surveillance, epidemiology, HIS	4
Pharmaceuticals, commodities & equipment	4
Human Resources assessment/planning	1
IDP & Refugee and Humanitarian Assistance Coordinator	2
Inspection-food, water and environment	1
Medical Service: capability assessment, planning and management	2
Health System Financial management	1
Security and Safety Officer	2
Public Information Officer-Communications Liaison	1
Logistics	2
Education	**12**
Institutional Capacity Building Expert	3
Vocational/Life Skills Education Expert	3
Refugee/IDP Education Expert	3
Social Service Support Coordinators	3
DEMOCRACY AND GOVERNANCE	**50**
Elections Advisors	3
Urban Planning/City Management	12
Human Rights and Humanitarian Protection	6
Anti-Corruption (Advocacy, disclosure, transparency, ethics)	2

APPENDIX D (Continued)

Conflict/Transition Officers	4
Public Administration	4
Leadership Development Specialists	2
Civil Society Advisor	3
Legislative Advisor	2
Media Advisor	4
Security Sector Reform	4
Rule of Law Advisors	4
Political Party Development Advisor	
TOTAL	**500**

Source: Suggested skills mix courtesy of Interagency Civilian Response Task Force, Office of the Coordinator for Reconstruction and Stabilization (S/CRS), U.S. Department of State.

APPENDIX E:
University of Florida
Land Tenure and Administration
Course Syllabus

University of Florida

SUR 6427 LAND TENURE AND ADMINISTRATION

http://www.geomatics.ifas.ufl.edu/courses/SUR6427/index-6427.htm

Instructor: Dr. Grenville Barnes
Room No: 406 B Reed Lab
Phone: 352 392-4998
Email: *gbarnes@ufl.edu*

Land (and resource) tenure provides a unique window into both social and eco-logical systems and is recognized as a key element in the battle for sustainability. In this course we will examine the historical origins of the idea of property and explore current land tenure and property issues in various parts of the globe.

Students will be required to read assigned references, review certain films, and attend and actively participate in class discussions.

COURSE OBJECTIVES

- To familiarize students with the range of current land tenure and property issues that are being faced in Latin America and elsewhere with respect to conservation, development, indigenous territories, common pool resources, natural resource management and gender equity.
- To critically examine development policy as it is reflected in approaches to land tenure and administration.
- To understand non-western approaches to property and how these are accommodated within western legal systems
- To familiarize students with processes used to formalize land tenure into modern property systems

CLASS PERIODS AND MEETING TIMES

PREREQUISITES AND REGISTRATION

This is a graduate level course that is designed to be interdisciplinary. No specific prerequisites are required, but students should have an interest in land and resource tenure issues. For registration questions contact Grenville Barnes at *gbarnes@ufl.edu.*

GRADING (SUR6427)

Class Participation.................10%

Short Assignments.................10%

First Draft of Term Paper......5%

Final Term Paper....................75%

CONTENT

1. Review of Major Schools of Property Theory

2. Roman Law, Civil Law and Common Law Systems (TA)

3. Overview of Land Tenure Issues in Latin America

    a. Indigenous Land Rights (JMR)

    b. Social Function of Land (TA)

    c. Human Right to Property (TR)

    d. Gender Issues (CDD)

    e. Poverty alleviation

    f. Conservation (Amazon)

4. The Mabo Case and Australian Native Title

5. Customary Tenure in Africa

6. Formalizing Property Rights

7. Evolution of Common/Communal Property Systems

8. Land Tenure and Parks (BC)

9. Land Reform (market-assisted vs state imposed)

10. Tenure, Resilience and Social-ecological systems

TA=Tom Ankersen; BC=Brian Child; CDD=Carmen Diana Deere; TR=Thomas Ruppert; JMR=Jerry Riverstone

BIBLIOGRAPHY

Adler, Graham. "Ownership Is Not a Priority among the Urban Poor: The Case of Nairobi's Informal Settlements." *Habitat Debate UNCHS— The United Nations Centre for Human Settlements* 5, no. 3 (1999). URL: <http://www.unhabitat.org/hd/hdv5n3/viewpoint.htm>. Accessed 24 September 2007.

Afghan Ministry of Urban Development (MOUD). "White Paper on Tenure Security and Community Based Upgrading in Kabul." Paper presented at the Conference on Informal Settlements and Tenure Issues, 15 March 2006. Kabul, Afghanistan.

"Afghans Protest Eviction of Refugees by Iran." *Hong Kong AFP in English — Hong Kong service of the independent French press agency Agence France-Presse (AFP)*, online edition, no. JPP20070501969040 Hong Kong AFP in English 0952 GMT, 1 May 2007.

Alden-Wiley, Liz. *Governance and Land Relations: A Review of Decentralisation of Land Administration and Management in Africa*. London: International Institute for Environment and Development (IIED), 2003.

Allan, Nigel J.R. Professor of Geography Emeritus, University of California at Davis, E-mail interview by the author, 16 May 2007.

ANIS. "Expulsion of Afghan Refugees: A Wave of Poverty and Unemployment." *ANIS (Companion) State-Run Daily Newspaper* (Kabul, Afghanistan), 3 March 2007.

Appaduria, Arjun. *Modernity at Large: Cultural Dimensions of Globalization*. Vol. 1 of *Public Worlds Series*. Minneapolis: University of Minnesota Press, 1996.

Augustinus, Clarissa and Michael B. Barry. "Land Management Strategy Formulation in Post-Conflict Societies." *Survey Review* 38, no. 302, ISSN 0039-6265 (October 2006), 10. URL: <www.fig.net/ commission7/geneva_2004/papers/lapca_02_augustinus.pdf>. Accessed 31 August 2007.

Augustinus, Clarissa and Dan Lewis. *Handbook for Planning Immediate Measures from Emergency to Reconstruction* (Peer-Reviewed First Draft). Ed. Paul van der Molen, Japp Zevenbergen, and Thierry Naudin. Nairobi, Kenya: UN-HABITAT Disaster, Post-Conflict, and Safety Section and the Land and Tenure Section, 2004.

BIBLIOGRAPHY (Continued)

Bäckstrom, Lennart. "Look at Ethiopia! A Simplified and Result Oriented Development and Implementation of a Low Cost Land Administration System." Paper TS-61 presented at the 23rd International FIG Congress, 8-13 October 2006. Munich, Germany. URL: <www.fig.net/pub/fig2006/papers/ts61/ts61_01_backstrom_0312.pdf>. Accessed 24 September 2007.

Ballenstedt, Brittany R. "Universities Propose Alternative to Public Service Academy." *Government Executive*. 21 May 2007. URL: <http://www.governmentexecutive.com/dailyfed/0507/052107b2.htm>. Accessed 4 April 2007.

Boguslawski, George. U.S. Army Corp of Engineers. Phone interview by the author, 2 August 2007.

Bose, Srinjoy. "Afghan Refugees in Pakistan: An Uncertain Future." *New Delhi Institute of Peace and Conflict Studies*, Report SAP20070226342002. 23 February 2007.

Boudreaux, Karol. "Property Holds Africa's Answer." *Enterprise Africa!* 23 September 2005. URL: <*http://www.enterprise-africa.org/publications/pubid.2449/pub_detail.asp*>. Accessed 8 January 2007.

Brady, Cynthia and David G. Timberman. "The Crisis in Timor-Leste: Causes, Consequences and Options for Conflict Management and Mitigation." Report for USAID. Washington, DC: USAID, 2006.

Cain, Allan. *Urban Poverty and Civic Development in Post-War Angola of Preparing for Peace Workshop on Future Swedish and Norwegian Development Cooperation with Angola*. April 2002. URL: <http://www.angonet.org/article.ph?story=20061116174108871&mode=print>. Accessed 13 July 2007.

Central Intelligence Agency. *The World Factbook*. Langley, VA: Central Intelligence Agency (CIA), 2007. URL: <https://www.cia.gov/library/publications/the-world-factbook/geos/af.html>. Accessed 2 July 2007.

Centre for Housing Rights and Evictions COHRE. "Global Survey on Forced Evictions." 2007. URL: <*http://www.cohre.org/view_page.php?page_id=10*>. Accessed 10 May 2007.

Cities, War, and Terrorism: Towards an Urban Geopolitics. Ed. Stephen Graham. Oxford, U.K.: Blackwell Publishing, 2004.

Cousins, Ben and Donna Hornby. "Land Rights: De Soto Solution Not for South Africa." *Business Day*, 13 January 2007, 1.

Cousins, Ben and Rosalie Kingwill. "Land Rights and Cadastral Reform in Post-Apartheid South Africa." Paper presented at the 9th International Conference of the Global Spatial Data Infrastructure (GSDI-9), 6-10 November 2006. Santiago, Chile. URL: <www.gsdi9.cl/english/abstracts/TS26.4abstract.pdf>. Accessed 24 July 2007.

Crossett, Barbara. "Misery Index of U.N. Panel Finds Africa Is Worst Off." *New York Times*, 5 July 2000. URL: <*http://www.nytimes.com/library/world/global/070500un-africa.html*>. Accessed 13 June 2007.

De Gessa, Stefano. *Participatory Mapping as a Catalyst for Rural People's Empowerment: An Overview of Experiences from the International Land Coalition (ILC) Network*. Rome: International Land Coalition (ILC), April 2006. URL: <www.landcoalition.org/pdf/mapping_ILC.pdf>. Accessed 25 September 2007.

Demarest, Geoffrey. *Property & Peace: Insurgency, Strategy and the Statute of Frauds*. Report for the U.S. Army, Foreign Military Studies Office. Ft. Leavenworth, KS: 2007.

Developmental Workshop. *Contributing to Poverty Reduction in Angola*. 31 December 2005. URL: <http://www.dw.angonet.org/>. Accessed 19 July 2007.

DiManno, Rosie. "Aid Groups Wearing out Welcome." *The Star* (Toronto, Ontario, Canada), 23 April 2007.

Dobbins, James, Seth G. Jones, Keith Crane, Beth Cole DeGrasse. *The Beginner's Guide to Nation-Building*. ISBN 978-0-8330-3988-0. Arlington, VA: RAND Corporation, 2007.

Dobson, Jerome E. "AGS Bowman Expeditions." *The American Geographical Society* (12 June 2007). URL: <http://www.amergeog.org/bowman-expeditions.htm>. Accessed 27 June 2007.

BIBLIOGRAPHY (Continued)

Dobson, Jerome E. "American Geographical Society (AGS) Conducts Fieldwork in Mexico." *Ubique — Notes from the American Geographical Society (AGS)* 26, no. 1 (2006).

Dobson, Jerome E. "Bring Back Geography!" *ArcNews Online by ESRI*, Spring 2007. URL: <http://www.esri.com/news/arcnews/spring07articles/bring-back-geography-1of2.html>. Accessed 18 July 2007.

Dobson, Jerome E. "Foreign Intelligence Is Geography." *Ubique — Notes from the American Geographical Society (AGS)* 25, no. 1 (2005): 1-2.

Dorpalen, Andreas. *The World of Haushofer: Geopolitics in Action*. New York: Farrar & Rhinehart, Inc., 1942.

Durand-Lasserve, Alain and Lauren Royston. *Holding Their Ground: Secure Land Tenure for the Urban Poor in Developing Countries*. London: Earthscan Publications Ltd., 2002.

Farah, Douglas. "Satellites Solve Salvadoran Farm Disputes." *The Washington Post*, 14 July 1996.

Fédération Internationale des Géomètres (FIG), The International Federation of Surveyors Commission 7, Cadastre and Land Management. *The FIG Statement on the Cadastre*. Copenhagen: The Surveyors House, 1995. URL: <http://www.fig.net/commission7/reports/cadastre/statement_on_cadastre_summary.html>. Accessed 24 September 2007.

Fella, Tim, Kim Jensen, and Martin Knudsen. *Consequences of the Formalization of Informal Settlements in Addis Ababa*. Aalborg, Denmark: Aalborg University, 2004.

Ferland, Yaïves, "Geographically Informed Structures (GIS) for Cadastral Representation." Paper presented at the 97th annual meeting of the Association of American Geographers (AAG), 1 March 2001. New York City, NY.

Fleming, Steven. Professor of Geography at the U.S. Military Academy. E-mail interview by the author, 10 August 2007.

Foley, Conor. *A Guide to Property Law in Afghanistan*. Oslo/Pakistan/Afghanistan: Norwegian Refugee Council (Flyktninghjelpen), 2005.

BIBLIOGRAPHY (Continued)

Foley, Conor. *Housing, Land and Property Restitution Rights in Afghanistan.* Centre for Housing Rights and Evictions COHRE, in press 2006. URL: <http://www.cohre.org>. Accessed 5 April 2007.

Foley, Conor. *Land Rights in Angola.* London, England: Overseas Development Institute, 2007.

Foley, Conor. "Legal Aid for Returnees: The NRC Programme in Afghanistan." *Humanitarian Exchange,* March 2004. URL: <http://www.odihpn.org/report.asp?id=2610>. Accessed 24 September 2007.

Foley, Conor and Ingunn Sofie Aursnes. "Land, Housing and Property Restitution after Conflict: Principles and Practice." *Humanitarian Exchange Magazine* (December 2005). URL: <http://www.odihpn.org/search_results.asp?page=3&searchtext=&keyword=Conflict&pubType=Humanitarian+Exchange+Magazine&region=>. Accessed 10 January 2007.

Food and Agriculture Organization of the United Nations (FAO). *Access to Rural Land and Land Administration after Violent Conflicts* 8. *FAO Land Tenure Series.* Rome: FAO Publishing Management Services, 2005.

Food and Agriculture Organization of the United Nations (FAO). *Land Tenure and Rural Development, FAO Land Tenure Studies.* Rome: FAO Publishing Management Service, 2002.

Fourie, Clarissa. *Best Practices Analysis on Access to Land and Security of Tenure.* Durban, South Africa: University of Natal, 1999. URL: <http://www.google.com/search?hl=en&q=Fourie+2B+Best+practices+analysis+on+access+to+land+>. Accessed 16 July 2007.

Frye, Timothy. "Credible Commitment and Property Rights: Evidence from Russia." *American Political Science Review* 98, no. 3 (August 2004): 454.

Galgano, Francis A. "A Geographical Analysis of Un-Governed Spaces." *The Pennsylvania Geographer* 44, no. 2 (Fall/Winter 2006): 72.

Galiani, Sebastian and Ernesto Schargrodsky. *Property Rights for the Poor.* Working Paper #249. Palo Alto, CA: Stanford University Center for International Development, 2005.

BIBLIOGRAPHY (Continued)

Gall, Carlotta. "Afghans, Returning Home, Set Off a Building Boom." *The New York Times*, 30 October 2006.

Gebremedhin, Yohannes. *Legal Issues Pertaining to Land Titling and Registration in Afghanistan*. Prepared by Land Titling and Economic Restructuring in Afghanistan (LTERA) Project for USAID Review. Kabul, Afghanistan, 2006. URL: <http://www.terrainstitute.org/reports.html>. Accessed 25 September 2007.

Geyer, Georgie Anne. "'Outsourcing' Is Not the Answer to Our Foreign Policy Woes." 23 August 2007. *Yahoo! News*. URL: <http://news.yahoo.com/s/ucgg/outsourcingisnottheanswertoourforeignpolicywoes>. Accessed 29 August 2007.

Goodchild, Michael F. "Geography Prospers from GIS." *Environmental Systems Research Institute, Inc.*, April 2007. URL: <http://www.esri.com/news/arcwatch/0407/feature.html>. Accessed 1 August 2007.

Hegland, Corine. "Pentagon, State Struggle to Define Nation-Building Roles." *Government Executive*. 30 April 2007. URL: <http://www.govexec.com/mailbagDetails.cfm?aid=36760>. Accessed 5 May 2007.

Hendry, Conrad. "China's Challenging Investment in Angola." *Hong Kong Trade and Development Council*. 28 March 2006. URL: <http://www.tdctrade.com/imn/06032804/investment037.htm.>. Accessed 19 July 2007.

Hespanha, João P., Mónica Jardim, Jesper Paasch, and Jaap Zevenbergen. "Modelling Legal and Administrative Cadastral Domain — Implementing into Portuguese Legal Framework." 2007.

Hillen, John. "Know Nothings: U.S. Intelligence Failures Stem from Too Much Information, Not Enough Understanding." *National Review* 50, no. 14 (3 August 1998): 1, 2.

Ingvarsson, Tryggvi Már, Tom Barry, and Margrét Hauksdóttir. "Reform of Icelandic Cadastre." *GIM International, The Global Magazine for Geomatics* 21, no. 3 (2007). URL: <http://www.gim-international.com/issues/articles/id867-Reform_of_Icelandic_Cadastre.html>. Accessed 27 September 2007.

BIBLIOGRAPHY (Continued)

International Institute for Geo-Information Science and Earth Observation (ITC). "Land Administration: The Path Towards Tenure Security, Poverty Alleviation and Sustainable Development." Paper presented at the ITC Lunstrum Conference: Spatial Information for Civil Society, 14-16   December 2005. Enschede, The Netherlands.

Jalali, Ali Ahmad and Lester W. Grau. Department of the Army. "Putting Humpty Dumpty Together Again." Ft. Leavenworth, KS: Foreign Military Studies Office, December 2001.

Jha, Lalit K. "Minister's Call for Aid Effectiveness Upsets U.S. Official." *Pajhwok Afghan News*. 21 April 2007. URL: <http://www.afghanistannewscenter.com/news/2007/april/apr212007.html#19>. Accessed 14 September 2007.

Jolie, Angelina. "Solving the Global Refugees Crisis." Refugees, October 2006. URL: <http://www.unhcr.org/publ/PUBL/4523cb392.pdf>. Accessed 14 November 2006.

Kaufmann, Juerg. "Future Cadastres: The Bookkeeping Systems for Land Administration Supporting Sustainable Development." Paper presented at the 1st International Seminar on Cadastral System, Land Administration and Sustainable Development, 3-5 May 2000. Bogota, Colombia.

Kemp, Jack. "Don't Forget Afghanistan." Foundation for Defense of Democracies (FDD), Copley News Service, 4 March 2003. URL: <http://www.defenddemocracy.org/in_the_media/in_the_media_show.htm?doc_id=160048>. Accessed 11 February 2007.

Kemp, Geoffrey. "Arcs of Instability: U.S. Relations in the Greater Middle East," *Naval War College Review* (Summer 2002): 61-71.

Leckie, Scott. "New Housing, Land and Property Restitution Rights." *Forced Migration Review*, no. 25 (May 2006): 52.

Lemmen, Christiaan, Clarissa Augustinus, Peter van Oosterom, and Paul van der Molen. "The Social Tenure Domain Model—Design of a First Draft Model." Paper presented at the FIG Working Week 2007, 13-17 May 2007. Hong Kong SAR, China.

BIBLIOGRAPHY (Continued)

Maines, Sophia. "Exploring the World Anew: Expeditions Touted as Modern Intelligence Gathering." *Lawrence Journal-World*, 23 October 2006. URL: <http://www2.1jworld.com/news/2006/oct/23/exploring_world_anew/>. Accessed 12 September 2007.

Mandel, Jenny. "Reconstruction IG Urges Interagency Coordination." *Government Executive*, 22 March 2007. URL: <http://www.government-executive.com/dailyfed/0307/032207ml.htm>. Accessed 12 April 2007.

Manwaring, Max G. "Defense, Development, and Diplomacy (3D): Canadian and U.S Military Perspectives." Paper presented at the Defense, Development, and Diplomacy (3D): Canadian and U.S. Military Perspectives, 21-23 June 2006. Kingston, Ontario, Canada.

The March. Starring Malick Bowens and Juliet Stevenson. Directed by David Wheatley. British Broadcasting Company, 1990.

Meha, Murat. "Effects of E-Cadastre in Land Administration in Kosovo and in Other Post Conflict Countries." Paper TS-50 presented at the 23rd International FIG Congress, 8-13 October 2006. Munich, Germany. URL: <www.fig.net/pub/fig2006/papers/ts50/ts50_01_murat_0392.pdf>. Accessed 25 September 2007.

Negroponte, John D. "Annual Threat Assessment of the Director of National Intelligence." Report to the Senate Select Committee on Intelligence. Washington, DC, 11 January 2007. URL: <http://intelligence.senate.gov/070111/negroponte.pdf>.Accessed 26 January 2007.

Nelson, C. Richard. *How Should NATO Handle Stabilisation Operations and Reconstruction Efforts?* Washington, DC: The Atlantic Council of the United States, 2006.

Nye, Joseph S. "After Rumsfeld, a Good Time to Focus on Soft Power." *Daily Star* (Beirut, Lebanon), 11 November 2006.

Nye, Joseph S. *Soft Power: The Means to Success in World Politics*. New York: Public Affairs, 2004.

Onkalo, Pertti. "Cadastral Survey Methodologies and Techniques in Developing Countries; Case Cambodia and Kosovo." Paper

BIBLIOGRAPHY (Continued)

TS-61presented at the 23rd International FIG Congress, 8-13 October 2006. Munich, Germany. URL: <www.fig.net/pub/ fig2006/papers/ts61/ts61_02_onkalo_0318.pdf>. Accessed 25 September 2007.

"Over 200,000 Afghan Refugees Said to Leave Pakistan after Deadline Expiry." *Associated Press of Pakistan (APP)*, online edition, no. 20070424950088 Islamabad APP in English, 24 April 2007.

"Over 3 Million Afghans Helped by UN for Repatriation from Pakistan since 2002." *Associated Press of Pakistan in English — government-run press agency*, online edition, no. IAP20070409950077 Islamabad APP in English 1250 GMT, 9 April 2007.

Pandit, Kavita. "Integrating Study Abroad into Geography Higher Education." *AAG Newsletter* 41, no. 11 (2006): 3.

Peters, Ralph Peters. "Out-Thought by the Enemy." *New York Post*, 1 June 2007. URL: <http://www.nypost.com/seven/06012007/ postopinion/opedcolumnists/out_thought_by_the_enemy_ opedcolumnists_ralph_peters.htm>. Accessed 24 September 2007.

"Providing Land Tenure Security in Afghanistan." *LTERA*, 2007. URL: <http://www.ltera.org/USAID_LTERA_LAND_TENURE. html#-Teaming_Up_With_the_World_Bank_KURP_Program_>. Accessed 7 August 2007.

Rajabifard, Abbas, Andrew Bins, Ian WIlliamson, and Daniel Steudler. "A Template for Assessing Worldwide Cadastral Systems as Part of National SDI Initiatives." Paper presented at the Global Spatial Data Infrastructure (GSDI) 9, 6-10 November 2006. Santiago, Chile.

Raza, Syed Irfan. "All Afghans to Be Repatriated by '09," *DAWN Group of Newspapers*, online edition, 16 February 2007.

Rubin, Barnett R. "Still Ours to Lose: Afghanistan on the Brink." Senate Foreign Relations Committee. Washington, DC, 21 September 2006.

Rubin, Barnett R. and Humayun Hamidzada. "From Bonn to London: Governance Challenges and the Future of Statebuilding in Afghanistan." *International Peacekeeping* 14, no. 1 (February 2007): 20, 23.

BIBLIOGRAPHY (Continued)

Safar, M. Yasin. Retired chief of the Cadastral Survey Department of the Afghan Geodesy and Cartography Head Office (AFCHO). Interview by the author, 10 March 2007.

"Second Generation Afghan Refugees Prefer Living in Pakistan." *Lahore Daily Times*, online English edition, no. SAP2007030527002, 5 March 2007.

Shannon, Elaine. "Can More Aid Save Afghanistan?" *Time*, 26 January 2007. URL: <*http://www.time.com/time/printout/0.8816.1582650.99.html*>. Accessed 18 April 2007.

Solis, Patricia. *Results from Advancing Academe: A Multidimensional Investigation of Geography in the Americas (AAMIGA)*. Unpublished report to the National Science Foundation. Arlington, VA: NSF, 2007.

Soto, Hernando de. *The Mystery of Capital: Why Capitalism Triumphs in the West and Fails Everywhere Else*. NY: Basic Books, 2000.

Stanfield, J. David. "Community Recording of Property Rights: Focus on Afghanistan." Paper presented to the International Association of Clerks, Recorders, Election Officials and Treasurers (IACREOT) 2007 Annual Conference and Trade Show, 19 July 2007. Charlotte, North Carolina.

Stanfield, J. David. "Land Administration in (Post) Conflict Conditions: The Case of Afghanistan." Paper presented at the World Bank Conference on Land Policies & Legal Empowerment of the Poor, 2-3 November 2006. Washington, DC.

Stanfield, J. David. *Privatization of International Development Assistance Stirs Resentment in Afghanistan*. Mount Horeb, WI: Terra Institute, Ltd., 2006.

Stanfield, J. David, Jonathan Reed, and M. Yasin Safar. *Description of Procedures for Producing Legal Deeds to Record Property Transactions in Afghanistan* in *Asia and Near East Reports*. Prepared under contract with USAID. Mount Horeb, WI: Terra Institute, Ltd., 2005. URL: <http://www.terrainstitute.org/pdf/Description%20of%20Procedures.pdf>. Accessed 24 September 2007.

BIBLIOGRAPHY (Continued)

Steudler, Daniel, Abbas Rajabifard, and Ian P. Williamson. "Evaluation of Land Administration Systems." *Land Use Policy* 21 (2004): 4.

Ting, Lisa and Ian P. Williamson. "Cadastral Trends: A Synthesis." *The Australian Surveyor* 4, no. 1 (1999): 46-54. URL: <http://www.sli.unimelb.edu.au/research/publications/IPW/CadastralTrendsSynthesis.html>. Accessed 25 September 2007.

U.K. Defence Geographic Centre, Geographic Research Branch. "Summary of Land Ownership in Afghanistan." Middlesex, U.K.: October 2006.

United Nations Economic Commission for Africa (UNECA). *African Geodetic Reference Frame (AFREF)*. 2006. URL: <http://geoinfo.uneca.org/afref/>. Accessed 12 September 2007.

United Nations Economic Commission for Europe (UNECE). Working Party on Land Administration. *Social and Economic Benefits of Good Land Administration*. 2d ed. January 2005.

United Nations Environmental Programme (UNEP) World Resources, the United Nations Development Programme (UNDP), the World Bank, and the World Resources Institute (WRI). *The World Resources 2005—the Wealth of the Poor*, 11, Ch. 3. 2005. URL: <http://multimedia.wri.org/wr2005/023.htm>. Accessed 31 March 2007.

United Nations High Commission on Refugees (UNHCR). *The State of the World's Refugees 2006 — Chapter 6, Rethinking Durable Solutions: The Search for Durable Solutions (2006)*. 2006. URL: <http://www.unhcr.org/cgibin/texis/vtx/publ/opendoc.htm?tbl=PUBL&id=4444d3ca28>. Accessed 25 September 2007.

United Nations Human Settlements Programme (UN-HABITAT). *Millennium Development Goals/Overview*. 2001. URL: <http://www.unhabitat.org/content.asp?cid=2799&catid=312&typeid=24&subMenuId=0>.

The University of Melbourne Department of Geomatics. *Cadastral Template*. Melbourne, Australia: University of Melbourne, 2007. URL: <http://www.cadastraltemplate.org/>. Accessed 12 August 2007.

BIBLIOGRAPHY (Continued)

The University of Oslo, the Norwegian Refugee Council, and the Norwegian Centre for Human Rights. *Norwegian Resource Bank for Democracy and Human Rights (NORDEM)—A Brief Presentation.* Oslo, Norway: 18 May 2005. URL: <http://www.humanrights.uio.no/english/research/programmes/nordem/>. Accessed 15 September 2007.

U.S. Agency for International Development (USAID). "Land Tenure and Property Rights Vol. 1." *Framework.* 2007.

USAID, Office of Conflict Management and Mitigation. "Land and Conflict: A Toolkit for Intervention." Washington, DC: USAID, 2005. URL: <http://www.usaid.gov/our_work/cross-cutting_programs/conflict/publications/docs/CMM_Land_and_Conflict_Toolkit_April_2005.pdf>. Accessed 24 September 2007.

USAID, Office of U.S. Foreign Disaster Assistance. "Shelter and Settlements Update: Afghanistan. Washington, DC: USAID, October 2006.

USAID and the Woodrow Wilson International Center for Scholars. "The Role of Foreign Assistance in Conflict Prevention." Conference report. Washington, DC: 8 January 2001. URL: *<http://www.usaid.gov/pubs/confprev/>.* Accessed 6 September 2007.

Van der Molen, Paul and Christiaan Lemmen. "Land Administration in Post-Conflict Areas." Paper presented at the 3rd FIG Regional Conference, 2004. Jakarta, Indonesia. URL: <www.itc.nl/library/Papers_2004/n_p_conf/vandermolen_land.pdf>. Accessed 25 September 2007.

Van Oosterom, Peter, Christiaan Lemmen, Tryggvi Ingvarsson, Paul van der Molen, Hendrik Ploeger, Wilko Quak, Jantien Stoter, and Jaap Zevenbergen. "The Core Cadastral Domain Model." *ScienceDirect* 30, *Computers, Environment and Urban Systems* (2006): 629.

Wertman, John. "AAG Washington Monitor." *AAG Newsletter* 42, no. 8 (2007): 5. The White House. *NSPD-44 Management of Interagency Efforts Concerning Reconstruction and Stability.* Washington, DC: TWH, 2005.

World Bank. *Urbanization.* 2007. URL: *<http://youthink.worldbank.org/issues/urbanization/>.* Accessed 10 September 2007.

BIBLIOGRAPHY (Continued)

Wright, Richard and Natalie Koch. *Geography in the Ivy League.* Hanover, NH: Dartmouth College, in press 2007. URL: *<http://www. dartmouth.edu/~geog/dc_geo_AG_WGI1.html>*. Accessed 15 July 2007.

Ziegler, Donald and Barbara Hildebrandt. "Advanced Placement (AP) Human Geography Testing Surges." *AAG Newsletter* 41, no. 11 (2006): 4.

Zimmermann, Willi. "Good Governance in Land Tenure and Administration." Paper TS.71-02 presented at the 23rd FIG Congress Shaping the Change, 8-13 October 2006. Munich, Germany.

ABOUT THE AUTHOR

Douglas Batson is a political geography analyst at the National Geospatial-Intelligence Agency (NGA), and is a staff member to the Foreign Names Committee of the U.S. Board on Geographic Names. He holds a Master of Education degree from Boston University, the German Language Diploma of the Goethe-Institut, and a Bachelor of Science in geography, earned entirely by examination, from Excelsior College in Albany, New York. He is a National Certified Counselor and previously worked in human resources capacities with the U.S. Geological Survey and the U.S. Department of Justice. Batson retired from the U.S. Army Reserve in 2004 following a career in which he was awarded the Bronze Star during Operation DESERT STORM and the War on Terrorism Service Medal following the attacks of September 11, 2001. His military schools include the Mapping, Charting, and Geodesy Staff Officer Course and the Defense Language Institute for Turkish. He has keen interests in the regional geography and toponomy of the Turkic-speaking world. This book is the product of his work as a 2006 ODNI Research Fellow. The author can be contacted at *Douglas.E.Batson@nga.mil.*

ABSTRACT IN FIVE LANGUAGES

English

Land is often a significant factor in widespread violence and is also a critical element in peace-building and economic reconstruction in post-conflict situations. This book examines how cadastral information (land and property records) can predict threats to regional stability, world peace, and national sovereignty. Beyond its application to the refugee situation six years into Afghanistan's reconstruction, cadastral data can also aid in recovery from natural disasters or wars. The book considers how causes of 21st century conflicts are related to land questions, and it introduces a new land administration tool. Significant inventiveness on the part of Lemmen, Augustinus, van Oosterom, and van der Molen has resulted in the Land Administration Domain Model (LADM). The LADM is compelling because it makes explicit various types of land rights, restrictions, or responsibilities. It is flexible enough to record both Western-style, registered land rights and customary, informal socio-tenure relationships typical of the developing world. In a word, the LADM aspires to address the myriad land issues faced by civil-military Reconstruction and Stability personnel in post-conflict societies. It merits close attention by NATO, the U.S. State and Defense Departments, and USAID because it represents one of the most important tools for countries where land administration has been weak or totally absent.

German

Land ist oftmals ein wesentlicher Faktor für das Aufkommen gewalttätiger Auseinandersetzungen und bildet ein wichtiges Element für friedensschaffende Maßnahmen und den wirtschaftlichen Wiederaufbau unter Bedingungen einer post-Konflikt Situation.

Dieses Buch untersucht in welcher Weise ein Kataster über Landbesitz die Bedrohungen für regionale Stabilität, nationale Souveränität und den Weltfrieden vorhersagen kann. Darüber hinaus wird gezeigt wie ein derartiges Kataster auch die Regeneration von Naturkatastrophen und Kriegen unterstützen kann, verdeutlicht am Beispiel der Rückkehr von Flüchtlingen nach Afghanistan.

Das Buch betrachtet die Zusammenhänge zwischen Land und den Konflikten des 21. Jahrhunderts. Zu diesem Zwecke wird auch ein neues Analyseinstrument eingeführt: die innovativen Bemühungen von Lemmen, Augustinus, van Oosterom, und van der Molen haben das so genannte "Land Administration Domain Model" (LADM) hervor gebracht. Dieses Modell betritt neue

Ufer indem es die vielfältigen Arten von Landrechten, Restriktionen und Verantwortlichkeiten explizit integriert. Darüber hinaus beweist es Flexibilität und kann sowohl für westliche Systeme offizieller Landtitel nutzbar gemacht werden als auch traditionelle und informelle Systeme, wie sie vornehmlich in den Ländern des Südens auftreten. Anders formuliert, das LADM strebt danach den zahllosen Landproblemen mit denen der zivil-militärische Wiederaufbau weltweit konfrontiert ist mit einer zentralen Lösung entgegen zu treten. Das Modell verdient die ungeteilte Aufmerksamkeit von NATO, den US-amerikanischen Verteidigungs— und Entwicklungsbehörden (USAID)—weil es eines der wichtigsten Werkzeuge für den Aufbau von Landverwaltungen überhaupt darstellt, und das insbesondere in Ländern wo diese nicht funktionieren oder gar nicht vorhanden sind.

Dutch

Land is enerzijds vaak een wezenlijke factor in het ontstaan van gewelddadige conflicten maar is anderzijds een kritiek onderdeel bij vredesonderhandelingen en economische wederopbouw in de omstandigheden na een conflict.

In dit boek wordt onderzocht op welke wijze kadastrale informatie gebruikt kan worden bij voorspelling van bedreigingen in regionale stabiliteit, nationale soevereiniteit en de wereldvrede. Verder wordt getoond op welke wijze een dergelijk gebruik van kadastrale data kan helpen bij herstel na natuurrampen en oorlogen. Dit wordt verduidelijkt met een voorbeeld van de situatie van vluchtelingen de afgelopen zes jaar in Afghanistan.

In deze verhandeling wordt nagegaan op welke wijze de oorzaken van conflicten in de 21e eeuw landgerelateerd zijn. Voor dit doel wordt ook een analyse instrument geïntroduceerd. De intensieve bemoeienissen van Lemmen, Augustinus, van Oosterom en van der Molen hebben geresulteerd in het "Land Administratie Domein Model" (LADM). Dit model is aantrekkelijk omdat het de veelzijdigheid van landrechten, restricties/belemmeringen in landrechten en gekoppelde verantwoordelijkheden omvat. Verder is het model flexibel genoeg om zowel de in de westelijke landen gebruikelijke landrechten als ook de gewoonterechten en informele rechten - zoals traditionele rechten in minder ontwikkelde landen te registreren. Anders geformuleerd: het LADM wil een gedeelde bewaarplaats mogelijk maken voor de talloze landgegevens, waarmee de civiel-militaire wederopbouw werkers wereldwijd worden gekonfronteerd. Het model verdient de aandacht van de NATO, het Amerikaanse Ministerie van Defensie en de Amerikaanse ontwikkelingsautoriteit (USAID), omdat het een van de belangrijkste hulpmiddelen van landadministratie vertegenwoordigt, en wel in het bijzonder in landen waar deze administratie niet functioneert of afwezig is.

French

Le terrain joue souvent un rôle important pour la violence répandue; c'est aussi un élément critique de l'établissement de paix et de la reconstruction économique post-conflits. Ce livre traite comment les informations cadastrales (les documents de terrain et propriété) peuvent prédire les menaces à la stabilité régionale, à la paix mondiale, et à la souveraineté nationale. Au-delà de son application à la situation des réfugiés après six ans de reconstruction en Afghanistan, les données cadastrales peuvent également aider à la récupération de catastrophes naturelles ou de guerres. L'argument examine comment les causes des conflits du 21ème siècle sont liées au terrain, et il introduit un nouvel outil pour l'administration du terrain. Une créativité significative de la part de Lemmen, Augustinus, van Oosterom, et van der Molen a produit le Model de la Domaine de la Gestion Foncière (Land Administration Domain Model - LADM). Le LADM est irrésistible parce qu'il spécifie les types différents de droits, des restrictions ou des responsabilités de terrain. Il est suffisamment souple pour enregistrer aussi bien les droits de terrain inscrits de style occidental, que les relations socio-titulaire coutumières et simples, typiques du monde en développement. Tout simplement, le LADM aspire d'être un répertoire pour les problèmes innombrables de terrain rencontrés par le personnel civil-militaire de Reconstruction et de Stabilité en sociétés de post-conflits. Il mérite la plus grande considération par l'OTAN, les Départements d'État et de la Défense des Etats-Unis, et par l'USAID, parce qu'il représente l'un des outils les plus importants en cours d'élaboration pour faciliter la gestion de terrain dans les pays où elle a été faible ou tout à fait absente.

Dari

ثبت نمودن زمین: ارزیابی املاک

خلاصه:زمین بیشتر اوقات عامل خشونت های وسیع است و همچنان یکی از مهمترین عوامل ایجاد صلح و باز سازی
اقتصادی بعد از زمان منازعات میباشد.

این کتاب معلوماتهای را که از ثبت املاک بدست می اید تحت بر رسی قرار میدهد که چگونه از تهدید به ثبات منطقوی,صلح
جهانی و حاکمیت ملی پیش بینی میتوان کرد. در طول شش سال باز سازی افغانستان از باز گشت مهاجرین افغان اشکار
است که ثبت املاک میتواند در بهبودی از مصیبتهای طبیعی و یا جنگها مساعدت نماید.

این کتاب نشان میدهد که جنگهای قرن بیست ویکم چگونه مربوط به زمین میباشد.

این نمونه اداره زمین نتیجه ابتکارات مهمی "المن,اگستینس,وان اوسترمبو وان درملن"میباشد.پلان LADM زیرا بلچسپ
میباشد که انواع مختلف حقوق املاک و شرایط استعمال و سولیتها را واضح مینماید.

LADM به طور کافی انعنا پذیر است که نه تنها قابلیت پذیرئ ثبت نمودن اسنادی که به طریق غربی ثبت شده را دارد
بلکه میتواند اسنادی را که در کشور های رو به انکشاف به طور غنغنوی, ارتباطات اجتماعی یا غیر رسمی مروج است نیز
ثبت کند. خلاصه اینکه LADM امیدوار است که یک مرجع جمع معلومات به ان مشکلاتهای وسیع زمینداری باشد که تیم
های بازسازی ونظم عامه در یک جامعهٔ رو به بهبود با ان مواجه هستند. LADM قابل توجه بیشتری NATO
وزارت خارجه ودفاع ایالات متحده امریکا و اداره انکشاف بین المللی ایالات متحده امریکا گردیده به خاطریکه یکی از
مهمترین وصیلهٔ حل مشکلات را به ان ممالک معرفی مینماید که اداره حقوق املاک در ان ضعیف بوده و یا هیچ صورت
ندارد.